Holy Spirit

Also by Ron Roth, Ph.D.

Books

The Healing Path of Prayer
(with Peter Occhiogrosso)

I Want to See Jesus in a New Light

Prayer and the Five Stages of Healing
(with Peter Occhiogrosso)

Audios

The Dark Night of the Soul

Healing Prayers

Holy Spirit: The Boundless Energy of God

Prayer and the Five Stages of Healing
(two-tape set and six-tape set)

(All of the above titles are available at your local bookstore, or may be ordered by calling Hay House at 760-431-7695 or 800-654-5126.

Please visit the Hay House Website at:
www.hayhouse.com
and Ron Roth's Website at: **www.ronroth.com**

Holy Spirit

The Boundless Energy of God

Ron Roth, Ph.D.
with Peter Occhiogrosso

Hay House, Inc.
Carlsbad, California • Sydney, Australia

Copyright © 2000 by Ron Roth

Published and distributed in the United States by:
Hay House, Inc., P.O. Box 5100, Carlsbad, CA 92018-5100
(800) 654-5126 • (800) 650-5115 (fax)

Editorial: Jill Kramer • *Design:* Summer McStravick

All rights reserved. No part of this book may be reproduced by any mechanical, photographic, or electronic process, or in the form of a phonographic recording; nor may it be stored in a retrieval system, transmitted, or otherwise be copied for public or private use—other than for "fair use" as brief quotations embodied in articles and reviews without prior written permission of the publisher.

Cataloging-in-Publication Data available
from the Library of Congress.

ISBN 1-56170-705-8

03 02 01 00 4 3 2 1
1st Printing, April 2000

Printed in the United States of America

I gratefully dedicate this book to my personal staff, with deep appreciation for all that they do through the use of their personal gifts, to assist me in accomplishing my mission to make known to the world the beauty, love, and power of God's Holy Spirit.

Just to be aware of the workings of
the Holy Spirit in our lives will lead to
an awareness of our own limitlessness.
For are we not, at the core of our being,
spirit and an emanation of the Divine light?

Preface

Reinventing Christianity

When I say that the goal of all my work—whether writing books or giving workshops and healing services—is to reinvent Christianity, some people think this is either blasphemous or downright presumptuous. Who am I to reinvent the religion of our forefathers? And yet the truth is that people have been reinventing Christianity for the past 2,000 years, almost from the time it began.

Just think of the sacraments, to take the most obvious example. Among the earliest Christians, the major ritual consisted of gathering in home churches and sharing a meal that became known as the *eucharist,* from the Greek for "giving thanks." Communion was almost certainly the first, and, for a time, the only sacrament in common celebration by the followers of Jesus. Baptism of new members into the community in memory of the baptism of Jesus by John the Baptist, public confession, the ordaining of clergy, last rites, the sanctification of weddings, and confirmation all followed suit. But in returning to scriptural roots during the Protestant Reformation, many reformers insisted that the only sacraments that actually took place in the Gospels were baptism, communion, and matrimony, and dropped the rest. Some dropped the very idea of sacraments altogether.

On an even more startling level, most modern biblical scholars agree that the first Christians, including Peter and Paul, expected Jesus to return in apocalyptic glory in their own day. That's probably one of the reasons why Paul had such a low regard for marriage. He didn't see any burning need to procreate if the Second Coming was just around the corner, and advocated marriage largely as a preventive measure against fornication. In various places in the scriptures, Peter makes repeated statements to the effect that Jesus will be returning soon, and the Letter of James (5:8) says, "The coming of the Lord is very near." If the Bible is the inerrant word of God, as so many fundamentalist Christians believe, how could Peter and Paul and James have misunderstood what would happen in the near future? Isn't it more likely that the first disciples' understanding of Jesus' message and intentions evolved over time, as happened with the followers of the Buddha before him and of Muhammad after him? Even the New Testament itself differs significantly in the Catholic and Protestant versions—the former including a half-dozen books that are not recognized as canonical by Protestants.

We could just as easily examine the doctrine of priestly celibacy still adhered to so firmly by the Roman Catholic church. As we now know, Peter and most of the apostles were married, as were many of the early popes. Until about the 11th century, celibacy among the clergy was either optional or not stringently enforced. But as the church amassed more land, it sought to prevent it from being passed on to the offspring of its clergy, and so began enforcing celibacy for economic reasons. Despite protestations to the contrary, the church's insistence on priestly celibacy is unrelated to the demands of ministerial life—as proven by the many thousands of Protestant, Orthodox Christian, Jewish, and Muslim clerics who have active ministries yet remain free to marry and raise families.

Continuing to more recent times, many elements of Catholic dogma—including the Assumption of Mary and papal infallibility—were not even codified until the 19th century. The Vatican Council of the early 1960s radically realigned the roles of clergy and laity, and introduced reforms so disturbing to some (changing the language of the Mass from Latin to the vernacular, for instance) that many priests, nuns, and monks left the religious life.

Like all genuine spiritual paths, when Christianity first emerged, it was geared to the everyday life of people. It helped them answer the burning questions of their day and deal with practical issues, just as Jesus had done when he originally taught what eventually became known as the Gospels. Jesus spoke of the lilies of the field and the birds of the air, and used metaphors based on harvests, food and wine, and servants and masters. He was talking to an agricultural society, and they understood what he was saying. But as Christianity advanced in years and became more institutionalized, its concepts became theologically more sophisticated, yet dealt less and less with practical issues.

If Christianity has been reinvented for all these centuries by everyone from breakaway reformers to the very hierarchy of the church, doesn't that mean that those of us in the trenches have as much of a right to do so? All spiritual paths are continually being reinvented and brought back to earth, and that is what this book aims to do—to return spiritual principles to their practical applications, stripped of their dogmatic baggage. Although I am a disciple and devotee of Jesus, I don't practice Christianity as it is presented today, especially in the fundamentalist version with its rigid beliefs and dogmatic practices, or in the rule-bound teachings of the Roman Catholic church. I prefer a path more in keeping with the Spirit of Jesus, which is the theme of this book. Part of my message is that you can follow the path of the Spirit of Jesus without becoming a member of any particular denomination.

What is of supreme importance is how the Spirit of Jesus manifests in each one of us. People talk frequently about "the human spirit," yet I'm not so sure that there is such a thing. Rather, it is the Spirit of God appearing within us in various frequencies depending on our thought patterns. If that Spirit is not allowed to manifest in an appropriate format, it will seek to express itself any way it can. I sometimes think that when people get up and cheer their team uproariously at a sporting event, they are doing so because they are not permitted to express their joy in most religious gatherings. I believe that many people also go to taverns and get high in various ways or engage in high-risk sexual behavior out of a need to express pleasure that is not allowed to be expressed where it ought to be primarily—in religious or spiritual surroundings.

Some Christian sects seem to act very emotional at their gatherings, but sometimes I sense that that's a cover for a lack of genuine feelings of love, joy, and peace. I'm not against spontaneous expressions of joy—singing, dancing, chanting—but I am against anything that appears to be excessive emotionalism. I get turned off when evangelists start jumping over lecterns, screaming, or throwing their jackets around. Some evangelists have recently begun a trend called "holy laughter" that to me is nothing but forced hilarity. Having been invited to appear as a Catholic priest on various Christian television programs, I've often been struck by the difference between the on-camera and off-camera demeanor of such evangelists and their crews.

John gives the best answer to this extreme behavior in his first Letter (4:1): "Do not believe every spirit, but test the spirits to see whether they are of God; for many false prophets have gone out into the world." As Jesus himself pointed out, "Not everyone who says Lord, Lord, will enter the kingdom." Jesus was more concerned with exploring spiritual depths than reveling in emotional highs. Excessively or superficially emotional behavior damages the credibility of the genuine message of Jesus. This is, in large part, what has turned off so many thinking people to the concept of the Holy Spirit, whose name is often invoked at these televised gatherings.

In evaluating the worthiness of different teachers and their presentations of the message of Jesus, you need, above all, to keep your objectivity. A healthy skepticism in this realm is not to be confused with cynicism. The key to making these kinds of distinctions lies in the way the Holy Spirit manifests in you, which is directly related to how you treat other people. All the actions of Jesus in the Gospels boil down to acts of kindness, compassion, or healing directed at other individuals or at humanity as a whole. But the churches have lost that orientation. In the Catholic church, for instance, when people are divorced, they are denied the sacrament of communion. Although the church touts the eucharist as the greatest source of strength and comfort, when people are most in need of it, the church denies it to them as a punishment. That's not "good news," as the Gospel is known; that's *bad news.*

And so if my interpretation of the nature of the Holy Spirit and how that Spirit works within us does not jibe with what the churches and theologians have taught over the years, I am not concerned. My mission, as I have said in the past, is to make God credible once again to the people who have lost faith in organized religion but still desire a spiritual life. I base my teachings about the Spirit on my own immediate experience of the Spirit at work in my life and in the lives of the thousands of people with whom I have shared those teachings and who have participated in my healing services. These teachings are not abstract statements, but have been road-tested. They are intended to make your life easier and more fulfilling in a direct way.

In his sermons, the Buddha repeatedly urged the curious to "come and see," to investigate his teachings and techniques for themselves, rather than to base their beliefs on faith. In fact, he often said "Don't believe me!"—meaning to try his system for yourself, and if it works for you, then believe it. I make the same invitation to all of you with regard to the teachings in this book. Don't be concerned about whether they correspond to what you may have been taught about the Holy Spirit as a child. Although I feel tremendous faith in the presence of the Spirit in my life and in the world, I don't expect you to begin with that premise. Rather, retaining both your objectivity and an open mind, see if what I have to say about the Spirit corresponds to your own experience, and whether the spiritual exercises I suggest help you live your life more fully. In the end, that's the only test that matters.

Author's Note: The Christian scriptures and most traditional theologians refer to the Holy Spirit as masculine in gender. Yet, throughout the Hebrew and early Christian scriptures, references to the divine Presence that represents the Spirit of God often use the feminine, as in the Hebrew words *ruach* and *shekinah,* and the Greek *pneuma.* Although God comprises both genders, the

English language requires a choice of gender for personal pronouns. Because I have come to think of the Holy Spirit as feminine, I choose to refer to the Spirit throughout this book as She or Her. If that makes you uncomfortable, feel free to substitute the pronouns of your choice.

A Healing Journey

Not long ago, I led a group of about 35 people from all across the country on a tour of sacred sites in Europe. They came together from different socioeconomic and religious backgrounds to visit locations from Prague to Assisi, with stops at holy places in France ranging from the supposed site of Mary Magdalene's burial to the place where St. Bernadette's uncorrupted body lies in state. At the prompting of the Holy Spirit, I had specifically chosen these sites because of my attraction to the saints buried there. I wanted to demonstrate to the participants on the tour that it is possible to tap in to the energy of those saints, as I described at length in my book *Prayer and the Five Stages of Healing*.

The most significant stop on the tour for me personally was a place in France called Taizé, the site of a unique modern spiritual community. Taizé was founded during World War II by a young man named Roger Schultz with the goal of creating a self-sufficient monastic community devoted to reconciliation among Christians. During the war, he used his house in the abandoned village of Taizé, near Cluny in Eastern France, to conceal refugees, especially Jews fleeing the Nazi occupation. Taizé is still going strong as a center of ecumenical renewal, and its innovative approach to liturgy and ritual has attracted a worldwide following, including a large percentage of young people from various religions. Visiting Taizé brought me back to my original vision of establishing a community of monks and nuns in my own neighborhood, men and women of all religious traditions, gay and straight, celibate and sexually active, who live in the world but who come together to pray and do spiritual practice, share teachings, and enjoy communal meals. My community would be centered on the teachings of Jesus, but would not be Christian as we understand that term today. The emphasis would be on taking these spiritual practices out into the world to live on a daily basis, as the people of Taizé do. Sometime ago, I had put the idea on a shelf in the back of my mind, but this tour brought it to the forefront where it belongs.

From Taizé we went on to Nevers and the tomb of St. Bernadette, where I held a prayer service. After that we traveled to Lisieux to visit the tomb of St. Thérèse, whose "little way" of childhood spirituality has been such an inspiration to me. All the sacred places we visited were uplifting to see, and the entire group seemed to be having deeply moving experiences there. Yet the moment we returned to our hotels, or went to board a train, we would be discomfited in one way or another. We had gotten off on a bad foot in Prague, where many of our party found that their hotel reservations had been "lost," or sold to other tourists, and so they had to stay at a somewhat less grand hotel down the street, although hardly a fleabag. Some of the people who were traveling with us were used to going first class, and at first they found this inconvenience disconcerting. One such couple, who were constantly being bumped to lesser accommodations, said to me as the trip neared its end, "We finally got it. If everything had gone smoothly and we'd had our deluxe accommodations all along, we never would have focused on the spiritual. We would have thought what a wonderful trip it was, but we would have been talking about our comfort. Now we know the trip was significant because of the presence of the Spirit."

I had to agree. In retrospect, the ten days of the tour seemed to be a metaphor for our individual journey from birth to death, focusing specifically on how to make the peace of God our only goal in life, and forgiveness our major function. From the beginning, the real subtext of our journey was not only to visit sacred sites and experience the energy of the saints associated with them, but also to develop our commitment to grow as the Spirit directed us. In the Gospel of John, the resurrected Jesus says to Peter, "In the past, you have gone wherever you wanted. But in the time to come, someone else will come and tie a belt around your waist and lead you where you do not wish to go." Some take that negatively, but I take it as the working of the Holy Spirit attempting to lead us through chaos to the goal of the peace of God. Chaos is there to let us know how free we are not when we want to control everything. Do we really mean it when we say, "All I want is the peace of God"? Or are we just mouthing a pious cliche?

The Holy Spirit constantly tests and tries us and urges us to wake up and do better. It's a little like those Zen masters who seek in various ways to throw their students into unfamiliar territory by short-circuiting the thinking process. They feed a monk *koans*—riddles that have no logical answer—to get the monk's mind to stop. In some cases, a master has been known to whack one of his monks with a stick or a sandal to get the student to wake up. The Holy Spirit also has ways of interrupting the thought process to bring us back to the present moment. Sometimes it's a riddle about our lives, and sometimes it's a whack.

On that trip to the sacred sites, a lot of us had to ask ourselves why we were there. We certainly didn't come to be inconvenienced, but neither did we come for a luxury vacation; we came to focus our spiritual energies. The conventional wisdom says that a major disruption in your life, such as the death of a loved one, a diagnosis of serious illness, divorce, or the loss of a job, can cause you to wake up and reorder your priorities. But I believe that the Holy Spirit also works in small ways, in everyday events, by shaking us up and making us ask better questions. If we can learn through flat tires and cancelled reservations to listen to the "still, small voice" within, then maybe we won't have to go through the big catastrophes just to learn the same lessons. Or at least we'll be better prepared for them when they come. There's an Arab story about a man who has a dilemma and asks advice from a wise older man. "I believe that God is watching over me," he says. "So if I tie up my camel at night, I'm afraid it will mean that I don't have enough faith in God. But if I don't tie up my camel and it runs away, I'll feel like a fool. I don't know what to do!"

To which the wise old man replies, "Trust in God—and tie up your camel."

What we all need to learn, and what I will try to show in this book, is how to balance the material and the spiritual in our lives—to trust God and tie up our camel. Too often people cling to one extreme or the other—either they are materialists and believe that, as the saying goes, he who dies with the most toys wins; or they become obsessed with the spiritual and forget that they're on the earth for a reason. Following the spiritual path does not mean denigrating matter, but learning to respect it without being overly attached to it. We have to learn to live with a foot in each world, but not forget about one world when we are deeply enmeshed in the other. One of the ancient Hindu scriptures tells a story in which the god Vishnu came down to earth and incarnated as a sow to kill a horrible demon named Hiranyaksha who was bedeviling the people. After slaying the demon, however, the sow remained quite happy with her new situation. Forgetting her divine nature, she grew contented suckling her offspring and enjoying the pleasures of earthly life. So absorbed was Vishnu in the happiness of his animal form that even the other deities could not persuade him to give up his sow's body and return to heaven. Finally, the gods sent the great yoga deity Shiva to reason with Vishnu. "Why have you forgotten your divine nature?" Shiva asked.

Through the sow's body, Vishnu replied, "Why be concerned? I am quite happy here."

Shiva then used his trident to destroy the sow's body, and Vishnu returned to heaven. Besotted by the pleasures of rolling in the mud, Vishnu had lost sight of the bigger picture. How could an incarnation of God forget His own divine nature? It seems impossible, or at least unlikely. And yet we all constantly tend to lose the ability to see ourselves as creatures in the divine continuum, rather than pigs rooting around in the mud.

Is there any way, you may ask, to retain our vision of the divine in the rough and tumble of everyday earthly life? For me, the answer is to learn to hear the guidance of the Holy Spirit, and then to have such confidence in that guidance that we don't hesitate to follow it. When we do, we can never go wrong in either material or spiritual pursuits. Learning to recognize the Spirit's guiding hand is half the game, and that's a large part of what I want to help you accomplish in this book. Before we can recognize the urgings of Spirit for what they are, however, we first need to know something of the Spirit and how She works within us.

Who Is the Holy Spirit?

In recent years, large numbers of books, tapes, workshops, and seminars have been devoted to previously undervalued concepts such as intuition, flow, guidance, spiritual healing, empowerment, motivation for success, and reinventing ourselves and our work. One quality these concepts share is the fact that, during humanity's thrust toward enlightenment, industrialization, and technology over the past three centuries, they have all been gradually played down in favor of logical thinking, rationality, a general speeding up of the pace of existence, and a disenchantment of everyday life. But these concepts also share a less obvious characteristic: They are also the work of the Holy Spirit. If we can begin to understand how the Spirit operates continuously in our lives, then our daily existence will become less stressful and more relaxed, filled less with drudgery and more with enchantment, and we in turn can become more creative and begin to enjoy a new sense of purpose, fulfillment, and enthusiasm.

Some readers may wonder, however, what helpful components of life such as intuition, motivation, and flow have to do with the Holy Spirit, which in the minds of many of us who were raised in a Christian tradition is associated with the Sunday school or catechism image of a dove, and identified mysteriously as the Third Person of the Trinity. I think we are still mystified by the Holy Spirit. God the Father we can understand; we can relate to His Son, Jesus, on a personal level; but who or what is that bird in the sky? Does the Holy Spirit have any reality beyond rounding out the Divine Threesome?

In fact, the Spirit has everything to do with the energies that impel us into more fulfilled and satisfying lives. It is the divine essence at the center of our being, but as long as we remain ignorant of that holy energy, it cannot be fully operative in our lives. Because of this, until we learn to recognize and then embrace the presence of the Spirit, we cannot be as productive, creative, and fully alive as God intends.

I found out years ago how dearly I needed to be informed about the workings of the Holy Spirit for my life to flow with increasing abundance on every level. Sometimes I'm a little slow on the uptake, but if I keep my mind open, eventually I get the message. When I left my last parish and resigned from the institutional priesthood, the diocese gave me a certain amount of time to find a home of my own, but I had trouble locating a place, and I was down to my last week at the parish house. As I worked with a local Realtor, I was especially attracted to one house, but I knew that I couldn't afford it, so I tried to put it out of my mind, even when the Realtor kept suggesting that I look at it. Although I often teach the importance of not putting limits on our thinking, I was guilty of doing so myself. I kept driving past the house, though, because something wouldn't let me completely forget about it. At the same time, I had been given a life-size statue of the Sacred Heart of Jesus by a parishioner whose wife was healed of cancer. It was a very expensive statue, but I almost didn't want to accept it because I had no idea where I could put it. I began getting a picture in my mind that when I found the house I was looking for, I would open the front door and see a niche where the statue would fit easily.

After driving past the house a number of times without going in, I decided to call the Realtor and have a look. I also invited a friend who was a member of the parish to go along with me. And when I opened the door, the first feature that caught my eye was a brick niche perfect for my statue of the Sacred Heart. Even so, I wondered how I could afford the house, which required more of a down payment than I could presently muster. Noticing the look of consternation on my face, my friend asked what was bothering me. When I explained, he said that he would help me financially so that I could get the house. As it turned out, it was a good investment all around, because the value of the house has doubled in the eight years since I bought it, and I was able to pay him back. Some people might say that was coincidence, but I don't believe in coincidence. I believe that this is what living in the Spirit is all about.

A similar thing happened when I was shopping for a new car some years ago. Because I'm big and tall, most of the models I tried didn't have enough leg room, and I struggled to find one where my knees weren't up to my chin when I sat in the driver's seat. All along I had been eyeing a Lincoln Town Car that looked like it would be plenty big enough, but once again I thought I couldn't afford it. After four months of trying to squeeze into smaller models, I finally gave up resisting and took the Town Car for a test drive. That night I realized it was the right car for me, and after I bought it, the money materialized to pay for it. The Holy Spirit had been whispering in my ear all the time, trying to help me overcome my resistance to getting what I needed, but I had pretended not to hear.

Once you learn to listen and tune in to the whisperings of the Spirit, you will be amazed at how much energy is freed up within you—because the Spirit is energy. At a time when spiritual teachers are increasingly working with energy as a healing force, we would be foolish not to examine this energy that has long been honored as the creative force of the universe, the very breath of all that lives. The energy of Spirit can assist us in our daily lives to be great healers, enthusiastic entrepreneurs, motivating speakers and teachers, great artists, innovators, or inventors. Just to be aware of the workings of the Holy

Spirit in our daily lives will lead to an awareness of our own limitless possibilities, for the very reason that at the core of our being we are Spirit, emanations of divine light. To be aware of the presence of the Holy Spirit will help alleviate the stress, tension, and sense of hurriedness that is already the cause of so much discomfort and disease in our lives. In place of that stress will come a sense of peace, harmony, balance, and tranquility arising from the knowledge that you are protected, guided, loved, and never abandoned. You will exude joy as your desires for success and fulfillment spur plans that seem to evolve from nowhere at the instigation of the Spirit.

Since the Holy Spirit guides us without our conscious knowledge, you may think it unnecessary to be aware of what's happening. Yet knowing that the Holy Spirit is at work will save time as you learn to trust your instincts, the "still small voice" that urges you to do one thing, or to refrain from doing something unhelpful that you may be about to do. As you begin to recognize that the Holy Spirit guides your actions and protects you, helps you remember things, and instills in you both desires and the plans to fulfill those desires, you will become more accepting of the impulses that spring to mind unbidden. Once you do, you can welcome the Holy Spirit's comfort, vitality, and enthusiasm, and begin to realize your visions and dreams.

Manifestations of the Holy Spirit

Because the Holy Spirit has been a fixture of Christian scripture since the earliest days, we should begin by looking at how Her manifestations were originally experienced. In his first Letter to the Corinthians in the New Testament, Paul describes a kind of division of labor for spiritual action, based on the various forms that the workings of the Spirit take within us: "Now there are varieties of gifts, but the same spirit; and there are varieties of service, but the same Lord; and there are varieties of working, but it is the same God who inspires them all in every one. To each is given the manifestation of the Spirit for the common good" (12:4).

In that letter and elsewhere, Paul goes on to list the different gifts, or manifestations, of the Holy Spirit. In Romans 12:6-8, for instance, he names seven gifts of the spirit, including prophecy, service, teaching, exhortation, contributions, aid, and mercy. In First Corinthians 12:8-11 and 28, he enumerates 17, including utterances of wisdom and knowledge, faith, healings, miracles, prophecy, tongues, interpretation of tongues, apostles, prophets, teachers, workers of miracles, healers, helpers, administrators, speakers, and the ability to distinguish between spirits. Five gifts are listed in Ephesians 4:6-8 and 11-14: apostles, prophets, evangelists, pastors, and teachers. And Peter adds two basic categories of his own in his first Letter (4:10-11): whoever speaks and whoever renders service.

Some of these gifts, such as prophecy, tongues, administrators, evangelists, and pastors, may sound overly ecclesiastical or outdated to modern readers. Yet if we view them in a different context, we can see that they are all workings of the Holy Spirit that can still have relevance for us. Evangelism, to take one example, doesn't have to mean only spreading the good news of the Gospel. It can mean being good news through our daily words and actions—in effect, spreading the gospel of tolerance and compassion. Everybody can learn to be good news, just as we can all learn to allow our enthusiasm to come forth (the word *enthusiasm* is derived from Greek roots meaning "God within").

Many people are confused about the meaning of the so-called gift of tongues. We see televangelists presuming to speak in tongues when they are merely spouting what sounds like made-up gibberish. But the original concept of the gift of tongues presented in Chapter 2, verses 4-13, of the Book of Acts has nothing to do with what is known as *glossolalia,* or speaking sounds not related to any earthly language. The Amplified Bible, which gives alternative translations (in parentheses) to certain Greek words to help the reader get a more complete understanding of the possible meanings of the text, translates the key passage this way: "And they were all filled, diffused throughout their souls, with the Holy Spirit and they began to speak in other (different, foreign) languages, as the Spirit kept giving them clear and loud expression (in each tongue in appropriate words)." That passage is clearly about speaking in languages that you have never learned but that other people understand as their native tongues. Although somewhat rare, there have been documented reports of this occurring in modern times, and it has occasionally happened to me. After one sermon I gave while still a Catholic priest, a woman approached me excitedly and asked where I had learned Russian. "I'm sorry to disappoint you," I said, "but I don't know Russian."

"Yes, you do," she insisted, and proceeded to translate back certain comments I had made in Russian during my talk. I had been aware of speaking an unfamiliar language, but to this day I have no knowledge of Russian.

What Peter calls the gift of service is also available to each of us in our own way. To be certain, not all of us are called to be Mother Teresa, but we *are* called to render service of some kind. Once again, the Spirit guides us to know what our calling is through the hunches, thoughts, or ideas that come to us in the course of the day. As you are walking down the street, you may receive a momentary impulse to buy flowers for a loved one or to pick up a used book for your child to read. That seemingly unbidden hunch to be of service may then be supplanted by the rational workings of your mind, telling you that you shouldn't be spending your money on flowers when you really need a new washing machine, or that your daughter probably won't read that book anyway. But the hunch came to you for a reason, and you have to learn to recognize such things—and to ignore the kinds of negative, rationalizing thoughts that often impede their flow or keep you from acting on them. You also need to learn the difference between the two, which takes time and practice. The Holy Spirit helps us to help others every day, even if we are not in a position to lead healing services or provide housing for the homeless.

The release of the spirit is accomplished by learning to pay attention to the guidance of intuition, which really means paying close attention to your thoughts and impulses. Much has been written recently about "soul," a part of us that comprises our mind, will, and emotions. But let's not lose sight of Spirit, which is the presence of God. As I have said, I don't believe there is something separate from God called "human spirit." Spirit is born of God and goes back to God. Soul is more like our persona; it is the manifestation of divine Spirit through the filter of our body. By this I don't mean to imply an erudite theological interpretation, but simply to say that Spirit is the essence that gives us life. Spirit wants us to accomplish certain things and so it fills us with enthusiasm. It is more than just our link with God; it literally *is* God within us. Which is not to say that we *are* God, but rather that God is acting in us and through us, and that "in" and "through" is what I mean by the Holy Spirit. Because we are made in the image of God, Spirit prompts us to create, although we create through our soul or persona. I may admire Mother Teresa, but my persona isn't made like hers, and so I serve in a different way.

We all have intuition, but few of us know where it comes from. As children, we were very intuitive because the ego wasn't developed enough to tell us to ignore the urgings of Spirit; now we have to learn to let go of those blockages so the pure essence of Spirit can flow again. That's what I believe Paul was trying to get across when he said that there is one Spirit but many manifestations. Take, for example, the issue of what we do for a living. The Buddhist concept of "right livelihood" holds that one's occupation should be such that it does not harm others and somehow contributes to human consciousness. But we don't necessarily have to make value judgments between, say, giving healing workshops or playing the piano, operating a family farm or running a comedy club. Entertainment and manufacturing can be legitimate fields of endeavor because they help people on some level. But within each occupation we encounter any number of ethical issues that require judgment, squaring one's individual vision with the demands of one's employer or of the marketplace. We all need to set boundaries in our lives, and the knowledge of where to set them can come to us through Spirit if we remain attuned to it.

Of course, staying in tune with Spirit is a large part of the endeavor of conscious growth. We have to learn to quiet ourselves to get into position to receive the transmissions from the Spirit that direct us in our right livelihood, among other things. Through prayer, meditation, and relaxation exercises, we can learn to open every part of our being to the knowledge and wisdom of the Spirit. Growing up in the Midwest, I became familiar with the story of Robert LeTourneau, who was one of the leading developers of earthmoving machinery in this century. LeTourneau is largely responsible for the increased size and maneuverability of such equipment manufactured by the major American companies. Although he never went beyond the seventh grade, he was a gifted designer whose innovations greatly improved the earth-moving vehicles used by the U.S. Army during World War II. Whenever LeTourneau traveled, he would take time to get quiet by himself while keeping an open notebook handy, in which he wrote down ideas as they came to him. In this fashion, he developed two enormously successful and influential corporations, and made a point of giving away 90 percent of his profits.

Most of us receive guidance all during the day, but we don't listen to it. Out of disbelief, lack of faith, or sheer inertia, we don't make a conscious effort to record and remember the ideas and hunches that come to us, and so they evaporate. Here is a brief practical exercise that can help you learn to remain open to the Spirit and take note of the intuitive messages of which you may often be unaware when your mind is preoccupied by other things. Because the workings of Spirit are rarely scheduled events, I have chosen to present the meditations and other spiritual exercises in this book as they occurred during the writing of the book or during the talks on which parts of it are based. If at all possible, take the time to do each exercise as it comes along. If for some reason that's not feasible, try to do it as soon after reading it as you can. Keep in mind that the Spirit interrupts you at different times of the day and night, including in your sleep, and that one of the keys to being open to Spirit is to take your inspiration on the wing.

Exercise: Breathing in God

Never go into this kind of exercise with the intention of "getting" something. Go in seeking God, and the rest flows from that. One thing I do suggest is that you get up early enough to do this before you start your day. I begin with a breathing technique to relax myself. All I do is sit for five minutes and become aware of the sensation of breathing in and out through the nose. You don't have to try to visualize anything, and if you're distracted, don't try to fight it. Just observe the distraction and let it pass. If you feel attracted to working with your breath, you can do a simple version of a breathing technique that, in the Tibetan Buddhist tradition, is called "pot-shaped" breathing. That name describes the distention of the diaphragm as you breathe in deeply through the nose and fill the lower stomach with air. You can even place your hand on your stomach and feel it expanding and contracting with each breath. Hold the air in for a few seconds before exhaling, slowly and steadily again, through the nose. This is not something to rush through like shaving in the morning. Just be aware.

As you take each breath slowly, you can begin to pray silently. On the inhale, think: "I am." On the exhale, think: "God breathed." Because I follow the path of Jesus, I like to breathe "Jesus" on the inhalation, and "Mary" on the exhalation. I use my traditional rosary beads to keep myself focused, taking one bead for each inhale or exhale, but you could also use a Buddhist, Sufi, or Hindu mala. As I move along the rosary, I may change over to phrases such as "God is" or "God is peace," and I often end with "Come, Holy Spirit."

This practice takes me between an hour and an hour and a half, and I keep an open notebook beside me so that whenever I receive guidance, I can easily write it down for future reference. If you prefer, you can use a small tape recorder for the same purpose. I recommend that you stop reading now, and try this technique for a few minutes.

Sacred Symbols

Some readers may wonder what immediate relevance the seemingly abstract theological concept of the Holy Spirit can have in their daily lives. But the truth is just the opposite: As opposed to the abstract theological concepts taught today by many religions, including many New Age belief systems, understanding the workings of the Holy Spirit is the most practical and results-based practice you can find. One way to get a deeper understanding of the value of the Holy Spirit is to examine the symbols for the Spirit that have been used consistently throughout the ages, especially in the Jewish and Christian traditions. The most prominent and frequently repeated symbols are fire, water, rain, wind, oil, the dove, and wine. Although these symbols may not seem related, they all have qualities that reflect each other in some fashion, and they all relate to ways in which the Holy Spirit inspires us.

The Spirit figured in both Hebrew scriptures and mystical Christian practice in the form of **fire**.

In Exodus 3:1-5, the angel of the Lord appears to Moses on Mount Horeb "in a flame of fire out of the midst of a bush." And in the First Book of Kings (18:20-40), Elijah challenges the priests of Baal to a competition in which God blesses the Israelites by spontaneously igniting their ritual offering of a bull. Fire from heaven also figures prominently in accounts from the Second Book of Chronicles and in Acts, when tongues of fire descend on the disciples of Jesus at the Jewish feast of Pentecost. Fire represents purification and trial, in the sense we still use of "going through the fire" or "baptism by fire." It is also a symbol of what we might call enthusiasm or zeal—being "on fire" with love of God or compassion for others. Fire was a provider of light and warmth from ancient times, and so one of humanity's most treasured gifts; the Spirit sheds light on us in a different way—through wisdom, intelligence, or intuition—but is even more to be prized.

In a similar sense, **water** has long been considered indispensable for preserving and enhancing life, probably because our bodies are composed mainly of water. In a dry land like the Middle East, water was especially valued as a source of life. In the Gospel of John (7:37-38), Jesus speaks of "rivers of living water" flowing from the heart of God. In the Book of Genesis, God creates water after He creates light. Throughout the Bible, water is conceived as the great carrier or conductor of God's essence: in the waters of the flood, the parting of the Red Sea, or the Jordan River where John baptized. Perhaps for that reason, baptism is acknowledged as the preeminent sacrament by all Christian denominations, who often have trouble agreeing on anything else.

Beyond survival, water refreshes us on a physical level through everything from a dip in the pool to a morning shower or a hot tub when we're feeling depleted. I don't think it's coincidental that people often sing or hum in the shower; something is going on internally as a result of the contact with water. In that same sense, by walking in the essence of the Holy Spirit, we feel refreshed on a psychological and spiritual level. The Spirit is life-giving water for the soul and the psyche.

When we speak of water, can **rain** be far behind? "May he be like rain that falls on the mown grass, like showers that water the earth," Psalm 72 says of the king. And the prophet Hosea writes (6:3) "Let us press on to know the Lord;

his going forth is sure as the dawn; he will come to us as the showers, as the spring rains that water the earth." The image of the Lord descending on humanity as revivifying spring rain after a long, hard winter is parallel to the image of the Holy Spirit descending on the disciples at Pentecost as tongues of flame. Without rain the earth cannot bear fruit or sustain life, and without creative ideas, we can't be productive either. The Holy Spirit brings those ideas to us to water our imagination, as it were, so that we can create everything from art and healing to entrepreneurial initiatives that sustain not just our lives but the lives of others. The urgings of the Spirit are not limited to "spiritual" concepts. Put another way, the spiritual must embrace the mundane aspects of daily work; service to others; creative art; music and writing; and creative business that respects other people and the environment. The idea that spirituality and business are somehow incompatible is not only obsolete, it's downright dangerous. At no previous time in human history has it been more important that business activities—from global communication to biogenetic engineering—be guided by ethics and respect for human life and the life of the planet.

"The wind blows where it wills," says the Gospel of John (3:8), "and you hear the sound of it, but you do not know whence it comes or whither it goes; so it is with everyone who is born of the Spirit." In that passage, the Greek word *pneuma* can mean either "wind" or "spirit." So, the **wind** symbolizes new revelations, creative ideas, hunches, and thoughts, as we find in colloquial phrases such as "the winds of change," "a new wind," or even "an ill wind." Just as a strong breeze replaces stagnant air with fresh air, so the Spirit brings with it freshness and new impulses to change our lives for the better, both materially and spiritually. Our ancestors, who survived by hunting and farming, had to be attuned to the wind and be able to determine in which direction it was blowing. Today, we must become attuned to the Spirit and learn to sense its subtle urgings—not merely to survive, but to prevail.

Because **oil** was traditionally used to anoint kings and prophets, it is an apt symbol of the Spirit's ability to empower us and bring out the most regal and spiritually profound aspects of our personality. Oil is both a good conductor of electricity (spiritual and earthly fire) and a symbol of healing, a balm, a salve. It is a facilitator that lubricates and removes dryness and prevents wear and tear and physical breakdown by relieving friction between moving parts. When people were anointed with oil in olden times, they were rubbed thoroughly, as during a massage. Today we are experiencing a revival of interest in the medicinal uses of essential oils. The French, for example, complement their medical practices by using aromatic oils for a variety of ailments. They employ oil of juniper to treat skin eruptions such as acne, dermatitis, and eczema; oil of lavender for flatulence and burns; and myrrh to counteract bronchitis and diarrhea. (For specific references to oil in the Bible, see 1 Samuel 16:13 and the First Letter of John 2:27.)

The **dove** has long been an emblem of peace, humility, and meekness. Today, the word *meek* has taken on a pejorative connotation akin to *wimpy,* but in its oldest usage it indicated the positive quality of having a mild temper and being patient under injuries, rather than vain or haughty. Meekness also implies the state of being teachable: you have to be humble to express your willingness to be taught because you know that you don't know everything. The phrase "meek the horse," for instance, means to teach it through discipline. The dove is the traditional symbol of peace, and peace implies balance and harmony. When we tap into Spirit, the essence of our being, especially through prayer and meditation, we experience balance and congruency. We are then able to be open enough to be taught both externally and internally by the divine Spirit. We become lifelong learners, recognizing that learning does not stop with formal education or job training but extends to every aspect of our lives. When we listen to the Spirit, we continue to learn about the role of diet, exercise, and good health; art, culture, and politics; and prayer, meditation, and spiritual practice. (For more specific references, see John 1:32 and Genesis 8:10-11.)

Finally, although it may not seem obvious or traditional, **wine** has often been used as a symbol of the Holy Spirit in both Eastern and Western spirituality. On a physical level, wine does bring joy and upliftment to the heart, and helps us forget anxiety and sorrow, however fleetingly. Because the Spirit will also do that in a more persistent and lasting way, scripture speaks of a kind of divine inebriation such as the one described in Jeremiah 23:9: "I have become like a drunken man, overcome with wine because of the Lord and His holy words." This equation of divine possession with inebriation from wine has appeared in other traditions, most notably in the writings of mystical poets such as the 13th-century Sufi Jelaluddin Rumi and the 18th-century Hindu mystic from Bengal known as Ramprasad, who wrote:

> *The divinely inebriating Goddess energy*
> *now permeates this poet so completely*
> *that common drunkards, soaked in wine,*
> *embrace me as their intimate companion.*

Because wine also makes us bold, it is an apt symbol of the Spirit pushing us to extend ourselves, take on new challenges, and confront dilemmas fearlessly. It may seem spiritually incorrect to suggest wine as a symbol of mystical experience in a time of crusades against drinking and drugs, yet when has the spiritual impulse ever followed popular or predictable lines of thought? Jesus seems to have perceived this very absurdity when he noted the response of the authorities to the quite different styles of himself and John the Baptist: "For John came, neither eating nor drinking, and they say, 'He is possessed.' The Son of Man came eating and drinking, and they say, 'Look, a glutton and a drunkard, a friend of tax collectors and sinners!' Yet wisdom is justified by her deeds" (Matt. 11:18-19). That last line suggests that Jesus knows that the workings of the Holy Spirit are played out in everyday actions that spring from the heart. Jesus healed on the Sabbath when the Spirit of compassion moved him; he didn't worry about the law. We can learn from his example that spirituality doesn't have to be legalistic, that discipline and inspiration can interact synergistically. Setting aside time every day for prayer and meditation is a helpful practice, but we have to remain open to the urgings of the Spirit at all hours of the day and night, even in dreams (perhaps *especially* in dreams).

In earlier times, spirituality was seen as part of everyday life, something woven into the fabric of daily work and play. The downside of that interweaving was that when the hierarchy abused its power, religion could become a tyrannical force, punishing free thought and nonconformity. But secularism, too, has a downside. In our drive to make life easier, faster, freer, and less driven by superstition, we have also removed any sense of enchantment from the physical world and distanced ourselves from the Divine. By being alert to the presence of Spirit, through Her symbols and their manifestation in our lives, we can draw closer to the Divine and reenchant the world around us. There is no reason why we can't integrate the spiritual into our daily lives without either ceding power to a possibly corrupt religious hierarchy or living under the taint of superstition. We can have technological and scientific advances, psychological sophistication, and spiritual power in our lives all at the same time.

The Magnificent Jewel That Dwells Within Us

Many years ago when I was a parish priest, I would sometimes hold up my chalice, which I designed myself, made of gold with a white enamel base into which are set the interlocked wedding rings of a close friend of mine and her late husband. Above the rings is a multicolored depiction of a flame representing the Holy Spirit. The congregation usually made appreciative sounds as I showed them the fine workmanship of this chalice and described its creation. Then I would remind them that at one time, the chalice was nothing but raw flecks of gold that had to be dug from the muck and ooze of a streambed. Those bits of raw gold had to be accumulated over time, then melted down and refined in the fire and pounded into shape by hand to fashion this beautiful gold cup to hold the wine for the sacred communion ritual.

That's what life in the Spirit is all about, because spiritual development is an ongoing process. You can't take a three-week course to enlightenment, nor can you ever think you've arrived and have nothing more to do. But by the same token, you should never be discouraged because you're not as far along as you think you ought to be. The spirit we have within us is a spark rather than a searing flame. Like the raw gold in the dirty streambed, it needs to be built up over time, then purified and refined and worked on until it glows. People look at the gold chalice as the finished product; they rarely think about all the labor and creativity that went into fashioning it. Writers like to tell the stories of spiritual masters who had remarkable enlightenment experiences that transformed them utterly. But those experiences, which may have taken place in a matter of hours, were preceded by years if not decades of assiduous work and prayer and attention to detail.

Some years back I came across a syndicated newspaper article that had originally appeared about 50 years ago. The article recounted the experience of a dean of the Harvard Medical School by the name of Dr. Cabot, who told the story in a speech before the Massachusetts Medical Society. Before performing an autopsy on a man killed in an auto accident, Dr. Cabot had been informed that this man had never been sick a day in his life. And yet through the autopsy, he discovered a surprising amount of scar tissue, showing that the man's body had experienced a number of ailments, including cancer, and had healed itself from all of them. At the moment the man perished in the automobile accident, he had several usually fatal diseases against which his system had begun to work to heal itself.

Dr. Cabot researched this phenomenon and went on to report his findings and his convictions that the body possesses an inherent wisdom that is biased in favor of life, not death. That is clearly good news to anybody suffering any type of physical affliction. "Most of the difficulty we have in our lives we never even know about or experience," the article states further, "because of the great healing process which is always going on. When we do come down with something, it is because that which works the revitalization within us has somehow broken down."

Such an assertion begs the question, *Why has the body broken down?* During his speech, Dr. Cabot asked the illustrious group of doctors he was addressing what we ought to call this powerful force in the body that is biased in favor of life. Then he proceeded to answer his own question. "We should call it God, because that's what it is," he said. "It is simply God. The healing power upon which we all depend is a divine healing power." He went on to say, "I earnestly recommend to those in the medical profession to let the patient know of this great force which is working with them. It does the medical profession no good to avoid the name of God. Tell the people the truth. It cannot harm them. Tell the people the truth."

About 20 years ago, the Christian medical doctor Richard Casdorf wrote a book called *The Miracles.* Chief of the Department of Internal Medicine at Long Beach Community Hospital, Dr. Casdorf became fascinated by the instantaneous healings of people with fatal or incurable diseases, and went on to research a series of healing miracles that had taken place among religious believers, primarily during services led by the

Christian healer Kathryn Kuhlman. Here are his conclusions:

> I'm glad to be a physician, and I believe God uses medical science to benefit humanity, but there are all too many cases to which medical science does not have the answer. Only those totally blinded by arrogant self-assurance fail to recognize our helplessness as humans in the utter need of Jesus. This is the day of the ministry of the Holy Spirit.

Dr. Casdorf became a great believer in the Holy Spirit as well. "The Holy Spirit is a person whom we must meet and experience," he wrote. "He not only empowered the apostles but spoke with them and guided their steps. He will speak to us and guide us today as he did in their days. The Holy Spirit is as active, if not more so, today, as he was in apostolic times."

Within every one of us is a powerful force put there by God, a force that works for our good. Like those flecks of gold in the streambed, it is there in nascent form, waiting only for us to help it coalesce. In the Old Testament, God clearly says that His plans for us are plans for good, not for evil. They are plans to bring us a future and a hope. The scriptures also tell us, "He breathed life into man," and we call that life force the Holy Spirit. In the midst of our sometimes desolate and depressed lives, we need to become aware that there is no reason for the human personality to suffer as some isolated victim unless we choose to, because we each have within us the power to overcome. All we need is the desire, determination, and discipline to release that power. When the Holy Spirit gets hold of you and you are aware of Her presence in your life, all things begin to change for the good.

When I truly know that a power greater than I dwells within me, which is the kingdom of God of which Jesus spoke, it makes me want to get up joyfully in the morning and spring from the bed. Of course, I have to make a confession, too. On some mornings, I say, "Oh, Holy Spirit, we'll just lie here together because I'm not quite ready to spring into action yet." But even as I'm lying in bed and am still aware of the presence of God, I feel hope communing with this presence called the Holy Spirit. As I go within and find that Spirit and develop a relationship with Her, that desire gets stronger and stronger. When I do finally get out of bed, I know I'm going to move my world. When I can apply that Holy Spirit to every area of my life, it makes all the difference between weakness and strength, enthusiasm and mediocrity, brightness and dullness, laughter and sadness, compassion and self-pity.

The Holy Spirit brings us out of those ruts. If you try to get out of them by yourself, you'll find that it's virtually impossible. But the Holy Spirit speaks into the ears of our heart and says, "You can be healed. You can be prosperous. You can become well. I'll show you the path to wholeness. Don't give up. Never give up, and watch the energy flow."

One of my favorite passages in the Christian scriptures is translated: "And the Spirit of God that was in Christ Jesus, that raised Him from the dead, is in you." But the Greek actually means: "There is a divine energy that raised Jesus from the dead, and that divine energy is in you." Yet if that same energy that raised Jesus from the dead—however you interpret that event—is in us, the only reason so many of us walk around with loser's limp must be that we have smothered the energy of the Spirit and drowned it like throwing a bucket of water onto a flame. We do that by thinking negatively, focusing on illness and on all the things that seem to be going wrong in our life. The moment we do that, we put out the fire and begin to go in the wrong direction.

We can also think of the Holy Spirit as a glorious, sparkling diamond in all of us, covered with mud and dirt and buried beneath the rocks by our negative belief patterns, just waiting to be dug out by changing the way we think. As with any mining operation, you have to go down into the darkness with your tools and pound away at the rocks and mud and slime. You chip, chip, chip, until suddenly you see something sparkle in the darkness. You really start moving now because you know that this is something you can get hold of. And after you have dirtied and blistered your hands in your desire and determination to get this diamond, you finally pull it out of the dirt and say, "I have found it!"

You don't believe what others tell you about you and your sickness; instead, you listen for what God says to you. Someone may say to you, "You're rotten, you're scum, you're no good!" and call you all sorts of dirty names. The more you think about it, the more depressed and sick you'll become. Then you may want to open up a sacred scripture and see what God says to you. "You are the salt of the earth. You are the city on top of a hill, the light of the world." When I hear those words, something within me begins to sparkle and radiate.

So when I go searching for the Holy Spirit, I chip away at the negative thoughts within me until one day I catch a glimpse of a sparkle. I listen to the Spirit of God direct me and guide me, and I follow that guidance until a miracle happens. A healing occurs—peace, joy, and love descend on me in a way that I didn't know was possible. Then it's chip, chip, chip, until I experience another healing, another miracle! Now I really want to live life to the fullest. Chip, chip, chip! Every day I chip away at the encrusted negativity that we might call *sin,* using only prayer and divine words of guidance, until finally my whole being is alive and radiant with the Spirit of God. (The Greek word translated in the New Testament as *sin* is actually a term from archery, *hamartia,* which means "missing the mark." I interpret Christ's use of the term to mean "missing the mark of love," since the greatest commandment in both the Hebrew and Christian testaments is to love the Lord your God and to love your neighbor as yourself.)

The Holy Spirit has made the most profound difference in my life. When I read what I consider to be positive scriptures, I do it with the Holy Spirit's wisdom. I may open up a book to read it and say, "I don't know what this means" or "I read this before." But with the Holy Spirit's help, guidance, and wisdom, all of a sudden the blinders are off my eyes, and I find something in a passage from scripture or from an inspirational book that I never saw before that I now can apply to my life with powerful results. Maybe I've read that passage hundreds of times, and it never made sense. All of a sudden, though, having finally turned more of my life over to the Holy Spirit, She revealed through Her wisdom what that passage can mean to me.

Sometimes we think that the Holy Spirit is something very complicated and mystical. Of course, Spirit is mystical, but that doesn't have to mean mysterious. The scripture says, for instance, "The Holy Spirit will teach you all things and will bring to your remembrance all that I have said to you" (John 12:26). Have you ever tried to remember something in a state of extreme anxiety? Psychologists tell us that when we're under stress we lose about 50 percent of our intelligence. That's why you can never find your car keys when you're late for an appointment and flying out of the house. But the moment you step back, get all those negative thoughts out of your mind, breathe deeply, begin to relax, and perhaps focus on a sacred word such as *peace,* you are able to quiet yourself. Then from down deep within you like a stream of water, something begins gurgling upward to your mind and you remember what you were thinking about or the truth behind it. That's the Holy Spirit.

I once heard a story about an 84-year-old man who used to take a walk every morning. One day as he was crossing the street, he was hit by a car and was killed. When they performed the autopsy, they called in the man's daughter and asked her how long her father had been ill. She threw up her hands and said, "He's never been ill."

"But when we cut him open," the coroner said, "we found his heart in such bad shape that he must have had several heart attacks." When she told them that he'd never had any heart trouble at all, they were incredulous. The only reason she could come up with to explain this apparent contradiction was that every morning he would wake up and sit at the edge of the bed, calling out, "This is *my* day! This is *my* day!" That type of positive attitude propels the Holy Spirit into work.

God buries the jewel in us, and we have the awesome privilege and adventure of discovering it and digging it out. That act on our part changes everything. We no longer look outside ourselves for help. When a problem or a difficulty comes up, we see it simply as a challenge, and we go within, asking the Holy Spirit how to work with this challenge. Then we listen for those thoughts, hunches, and ideas to come to us. They may not always come when we desire; they may come at moments when the mind is at rest—in the shower, driving the car, lying down, or meditating.

When I lay hands upon people at a healing service, or the Holy Spirit begins to reveal to me through an intuitive "hit" that a particular ailment is being healed, I see or feel it taking place. If God says that He has put within us a Spirit of Holiness and Wholeness, I'm stupid enough to believe this—and in the process I have moved mountains. In the Book of Acts, Peter says, "And you no doubt know that Jesus of Nazareth was anointed by God with the Holy Spirit and with power. He went around doing good and healing all, for God was with him." Even as Peter was saying these things, the Holy Spirit fell upon all those who were listening. The Jews who came with Peter were amazed that the gift of the Holy Spirit would be given to the gentiles as well.

The power of God, the only power that can work miracles in your life, is within you, whatever your religion, nationality, sexual preference, gender, or race. Stop quenching it; stop grieving the Holy Spirit by wondering what others will say or think if they find out that you love the Holy Spirit. I'll tell you what they will do—they will faint in your presence because you will possess a new zest for living, a new passion, and a new freedom that they never dreamed possible.

The Spirit of the Lord Is Upon Me:

Eight Signs to Expect from the Spirit

The life of Jesus of Nazareth demonstrates that it is possible for all sons and daughters of God to express their divinity. In his words and actions, Jesus embodied the image of someone operating at the highest level of spiritual realization. In the 4th chapter of the Gospel of Luke, Jesus has just been baptized in the River Jordan, and the Holy Spirit in the form of a dove has descended upon him. Energized by the Spirit, Jesus is led into the desert, where he encounters a series of temptations that are recognizable as the urgings of the ego to use the considerable spiritual powers loosed by his enlightenment in the Jordan for selfish or self-aggrandizing purposes. According to the 14th verse of Luke, Jesus returns to Galilee "in the power of the Holy Spirit." When he enters the temple, he is handed the scroll of the Prophet Isaiah, and, unrolling it, he finds the place where these words are written:

> *The Spirit of the Lord God is upon*
> *me, because he has anointed me to preach*
> *good news to the humble;*
> *He has set me to proclaim release for*
> *the captives, and the recovery of sight*
> *to the blind, to liberate the oppressed;*
> *and to proclaim the year of the Lord's favor.*

When I began to meditate on this passage, I wanted to form a picture in my mind of how Jesus would have approached this scenario. It was a custom of the Jewish people of that era to call on one of the men in the congregation to come up, take a passage, and expound some truth to share with the people. On this particular day, Jesus was chosen to come up and teach. Led by the Spirit of God, he opened to the passage of Isaiah and became very excited when he read those words. If he were reading them today, he might have added a gloss: "The Lord has sent me to proclaim freedom for the prisoners, not just those in jail cells but those imprisoned in their negative thoughts. He has sent me to offer recovery of sight to the blind, not only the physically blind but the spiritually blind, too. Anything that is coming against you, anything that you feel is a trial and tribulation, this day you can forget it because the Spirit of the Lord God has called me to set you free."

All eyes were upon him. It got perfectly still in the assembly, and in that quietness, Jesus said, "Today this scripture has been fulfilled." Bombshell! You can only imagine what the response might have been in a small-town congregation like that. Jesus was saying outright that he came there because he had been anointed by the Spirit. Although the people received him well at first, the more Jesus spoke, the angrier they grew, until they finally chased him from the synagogue and tried to stone him. All this because he had said that he was anointed by the Holy Spirit!

The good news is that you, too, are anointed, if only you open up to the Spirit. Then you will be able to say the same words: "The Spirit of the Lord God, the very breath of life, is upon me." The words of Isaiah as they appear in Luke's Gospel are slightly different from the complete text of Isaiah 61:1-4. Here are the exact words as they appear in the Hebrew scroll from which Jesus would have been reading:

> *The Spirit of the Lord God is upon me,*
> *because the Lord has anointed me to preach*
> *good news to the humble.*
> *He has sent me to bind up the broken hearted,*
> *to proclaim freedom for the captives,*
> *and release from darkness for the prisoners;*
> *to proclaim the year of the Lord's favor, . . .*
> *to comfort all who mourn and provide*
> *for those who grieve in Zion—*
> *to bestow upon them a crown*
> *of beauty instead of ashes, the oil*
> *of gladness instead of mourning, a garment*
> *of praise instead of a spirit of despair.*
> *They will be called oaks of holiness*
> *(wholeness), a planting of the*
> *Lord for the display of His splendor.*

Once we welcome this great anointing of the Holy Spirit into our lives, Isaiah is saying, a radiance and a light will grow within us that will reflect the glory of God. The Lord doesn't want us to be objects of despair, walking around with loser's limp, which is the normal human condition. The Lord wants us to be oaks of holiness, of wholeness, that reflect His glory. A sad person does not glorify God, and the sadder we get, the sicker we become. So God has sent us the breath of life, the Holy Spirit, to pull us out of the doldrums of apathy and self-pity that we get ourselves into. The Spirit of the Lord God is upon us to set us free so that we can set others free. God never gives us His Spirit for ourselves alone. In fact, if we approach God for His spirit with ourselves mainly in mind, I believe that He withholds the vast majority of this breath of life even though He wants us to be full. I believe this because humility is a prerequisite for us to keep walking permanently in the fullness of the Spirit.

Jesus knew that he had been anointed by the Spirit because, well, he *knew*. What about the rest of us? I've already advised you to learn to trust your intuition; to listen for the still, small voice; and to distinguish between the positive and negative input you get from those around you. But there are other signs that we can expect when the Holy Spirit is upon us and we permit Her to work through us. Some are self-explanatory, and some require more explanation, so I'll take them one at a time. This list is not meant to be exhaustive, but simply to help you cultivate awareness of Spirit and develop the knack of living in the present moment.

1. We can expect that the Spirit will convince us that our life isn't as fulfilling as we think it is.

Some people in religious circles call that conviction, but conviction sounds negative. The Spirit shows us, saying, for example, "Ron, come here. Sit down a minute. Look at this—this impatience, this anger, this hostility, this bitterness."

"Oh, yeah, I see that. I thought I got rid of that ten years ago."

"No, you didn't. It's still there."

The Spirit begins by convincing us that our life could be better, that we have not yet arrived. Don't believe that beer commercial that says, "It doesn't get any better than this." It does, when the Spirit of God is upon us.

2. We can expect that the Holy Spirit will always point to the Divine.

God will no longer be an abstraction; He will be real. You will sense His embrace and love, and you will hear Him say to you, "I love you. Come and take my hand. I will show you how to be a conqueror in life no matter what comes against you." The Holy Spirit directs you to stop beating yourself up with a sense of unworthiness, because that does not give God glory. Teresa of Avila, the 16th-century Spanish mystic who founded a reformed order of nuns called the Discalced (or Barefoot) Carmelites, put it this way: "Those souls who have reached to a perfect union with God hold themselves in high esteem with a humble and holy presumption." God doesn't want us to think ill of ourselves or to believe that we're nothing. To be confident, you don't need to be cocky; to be humble, you don't need to put yourself down. When we are able to walk in confidence, we are humble enough to know that it's God's power, not ours. It's God's wisdom, God's understanding, and God's love, not ours. For example, there are some people we truly don't care for, but God's strength and love give us a new perception so that we can love them anyway.

3. When the Holy Spirit is upon us, we are filled with life, where once there was death and

darkness because of resentment, bitterness, anger, and hostility.

The Spirit feeds us with the healing balm of light. We call it love, peace, and joy. Unless we open up to the Spirit and receive Her forgiveness and pass it on, we will never become men and women of holiness. We will never radiate the presence of God. Forgiveness is the heart of Jesus' message. Every time we are tempted to look back at something yesterday, 10 years ago, or 40 years ago, we can remember that Jesus embraced us at one moment and said, "That's forgiven. You came to me, and I took care of that. Now stop thinking about it." Put your focus on God's love for you; the more you do that, the more you will be embraced with the radiance that no one will ever take from you.

4. When the Holy Spirit is upon us, She sets us free.

Real freedom doesn't mean trampling on people and getting what you want at any cost. Real freedom is inside you. You wake up in the morning and you're filled with an enthusiasm and a zest for life you never had before, and you say, "I don't know what this is." It's the Holy Spirit.

You wake up in the morning, and you're ready to get on with life. That's the Holy Spirit setting you free. You feel like you're a sailboat out on the lake somewhere, and a great breath of wind is pumping up your sails, helping you glide along the waves. That's what this life is all about. Every now and then a storm will rise up, but when it comes, you have to keep your focus on God's Spirit within you, not on the storm.

A medical doctor once asked me, "How can I have the divine more in my life?"

I told him to pray for his patients. "You don't have to stand there and say, 'Get ready now. I'm going to pray for you,'" I said. "But as you are listening to them tell you about their aches and ailments, just say silently 'Come, Holy Spirit.'"

I told him to do that because it's what I do. When I'm talking with people who come to me for guidance and counseling, under my breath I'll say, "Come, Holy Spirit," because I want the Spirit to minister to them. I often don't know what to say to people, but the Spirit does. The Spirit knows what they need. So under your breath, you too can say, "Come, Holy Spirit" and let Her initiate this time of ministry and healing.

The 16th chapter of the Gospel of Mark reads: "Later, Jesus appeared to the eleven as they were eating. He rebuked them for their lack of faith and their stubborn refusal to believe those who had seen him after he had risen." If you think that God as your divine Mother or Father will never slap your wrist, think again. Unconditional love doesn't mean being afraid to tell your loved ones when you believe they're on the wrong track. Jesus said to his followers, "Go into all the world and demonstrate the good news to all creation." That means whatever your world is—doctor, minister, teacher, homemaker, plumber, or waitress—ask for the Holy Spirit to use that job to minister to others. When you pray for yourself, remember that you must pray first for this empowering of the Holy Spirit to minister God's love to others and set them free. In the process of that giving, you will be set free yourself. Sometimes we have it backwards. We want to get first and then we'll give, but it doesn't work that way. For this reason, I suggest that you pray for the sick on a regular basis in your daily devotions.

When I was still a Catholic priest, I was invited to lead a service outside of my home parish, in Joliet, Illinois. About 45 minutes before the service was due to begin, the church was already almost full, and I was pacing back and forth. The assistant pastor said to me, "Father, you're almost ready to go out, and it looks like you're going to have a full church—might be standing room only."

"Yes," I said, and kept walking back and forth.

"You aren't nervous, are you?" he asked.

"Yes, I am."

"Well, how long have you been doing this?"

"Fourteen years."

"Don't you ever stop getting nervous?"

"I haven't yet," I said. The reason is that a part of me wants to plan this whole thing so when I go out there, I will do it my way. But another part of me says, "Come, Holy Spirit. You know what they need tonight, and I don't." The Spirit tells me "Do this," and I do it. It's a beautiful way to live, but it does make you a little nervous if you are used to manipulating people and controlling situations. I assured this assistant pastor that I didn't think my nervousness would ever end, and if it did, then I probably ought to get back on my knees and ask God why. Because then it sounds as if I know everything that is going to happen and I'm in charge again. But I don't want to be in charge. The only way I can be in charge of my life is by letting the Spirit of God be upon me to guide me.

5. When the Holy Spirit is upon us, She forms the Christ nature within us.

The Christ nature is not about miraculous power, but about love, first and foremost. In the Book of Acts is a wonderful statement attributed to Jesus that most theologians tend to ignore: "And after the Holy Spirit comes upon you, you shall receive power." That line indicates that first comes the Presence, the love, and then the power flows from that. That's why all the forms of silent prayer and meditation are so essential—they teach you how to quiet your mind so that you can experience the Presence of God. The enthusiasm that follows that experience—the bliss or ecstacy that some mystics have described—is nothing more than the vibration of the body receiving power. That's why people who have a passion for what they do emanate power and charisma; the force of their teaching or performance comes from their passion, which is a form of love.

We always need to balance power and love. We refer to the healings and other inexplicable acts of Jesus as *miracles*, and the Bible calls them "signs and wonders," but they were all acts of love that flowed from the great compassion of Jesus. His transformation of water into wine at the wedding feast of Cana was not a parlor trick to display his powers, but was done out of compassion for the married couple so that they would not be humiliated at having run out of wine. When Jesus calmed the storm on the Sea of Galilee, he was feeling compassion for his frightened disciples. And the same is clearly true of his miraculous healings: They weren't intended, as some Christians insist, to prove that Jesus was God. They were direct expressions of his love for people. The Christ nature that the Holy Spirit forms within us if we allow Her to work is first and foremost our ability to express love; if that passion then endows us with the power to help others, that is a secondary result.

6. The Holy Spirit guides those who trust in Her.

It doesn't matter who you are, because we all need to grow in trust, and trust begins by knowing that God loves us.

7. We become thankful worshipers of the Mother.

We want to praise Her and to give Her glory and tell Her, "I love you, Father/Mother."

8. We feel empowered to serve others.

Everybody today wants to be a leader, to be number one, but very few are willing to scrub the toilets and floors to get there. That's a little like the old blues song, "Everybody Wants to Go to Heaven, But Nobody Wants to Die." Yet God demands that you start out with the little things, and when you're faithful in that arena, He will give you the big things to do. God empowers us for service to advance the awareness of His love for all creation, but He generally takes it one step at a time.

Once you become aware of that—and it won't happen overnight—you will be able to say with Jesus, "The Spirit of the Lord God is upon *me.* He has anointed *me* with joy and with an oil of gladness that calls *me* to be good news to others, to set people free so they can celebrate life to the fullest." God has never called us into mere existence. He has called us into celebration of life, and until you know that and experience that, you will never fully understand the Holy Spirit, Her personality, or Her works.

The Gifts and the Fruit of the Holy Spirit

The manifestations of the Holy Spirit in our lives can probably best be gathered into two basic groups: the gifts of the Spirit and the fruit of the Spirit. The gifts are the more readily apparent of the two, including spontaneous healings, prophecy, talking in tongues, ecstatic states, bilocation (the ability to be in two places at once), and brief lapses into unconsciousness known as "resting in the Spirit." Commonly referred to in the Christian tradition as gifts of power, or "signs and wonders," some of these resemble the manifestations known in the Hindu tradition of India as *siddhis*, or psychic powers. And just as spiritual masters of the East warn their students to beware of the distraction of achieving siddhis without first being grounded in prayer and self-control, I always caution people not to get caught up in pursuing the *gifts* of the Spirit without their being balanced by the *fruit* of the Spirit. Otherwise, you run the risk of being destroyed by the very powers you are seeking. The gifts of the Spirit also include certain natural graces, however, that are quite distinct from the "supernatural" gifts just mentioned, and I will discuss those in a moment.

The more subtle fruit of the Spirit, according to St. Paul, is "love, joy, peace, patience, kindness, goodness, faithfulness, gentleness, and self-control," although those can easily be boiled down to one attribute from which all the rest flow: *love*. Some Christian groups tend to focus on the power and miss the love. If you focus on the love, however, you won't miss the power. And yet because the fruit is less apparent than the gifts, it is easy to overlook. I will discuss the fruit of the Spirit as characterized by unconditional love in the next section of this book, but first I would like to focus on the gifts because they are so often misunderstood and so widely misrepresented.

When it comes to the so-called supernatural gifts, one may rightly ask if God would create gifts that could actually cause problems for us.

The closest parallel I can think of is fire, which is universally considered a great gift that made it possible for the earliest humans to stay warm through cold winters and to migrate from the tropical zones where human life began; to cook food; and ultimately to advance as a civilization. And yet if fire isn't properly controlled, it can be one of the most destructive forces on earth. If you play with fire, as the saying goes, you'll get burned. Electricity is a highly refined form of fire that has totally transformed human society, and yet it, too, can cause tremendous harm. And nuclear power, the most potent extension of fire that we know, has the potential, if misused, to completely obliterate human life.

That's why balance is so crucial in the life of the Spirit. Power is a necessary part of our life, but unless it's tempered by the fruit—love—we can't be whole. If we focus only on power or only on love, we will not have a whole spiritual life. The Tibetan Buddhists speak of wisdom and compassion as the two wings of an eagle necessary to soar above the clouds. If you practice wisdom without compassion, you end up at best like an enlightened despot. But it's equally destructive to practice compassion without wisdom, as in continually giving money to people rather than teaching them a trade. By balancing wisdom and compassion, the enlightened being employs what the Buddhists refer to as "skillful means" to lead others to spiritual realization.

Perhaps even more important than the gifts that can be termed "signs and wonders," however, are the natural graces mentioned in several places in scripture. Paul's Letter to the Romans lists seven gifts of the Spirit: prophecy, service, teaching, exhortation, contributions, aid, and mercy. As mentioned earlier, his Letter to the Corinthians mentions 17, including the utterance of wisdom and knowledge, faith, healings, miracles, prophecy, the ability to distinguish between spirits, tongues, interpretation of tongues, apostles, prophets, teachers, workers of miracles, healers, helpers, and administrators. And the First Letter of Peter distinguishes two categories: whoever speaks and whoever renders service. Many of those categories, as you can readily see, include graces and predispositions that need to be developed. As gifted with natural athletic graces as someone like Michael Jordan might be, for instance, he could not have developed into the great star he was without discipline and hard work. You may be graced with a natural gift for teaching, administrating, or healing, but you won't go very far with it if you don't practice it and discipline yourself. What the Holy Spirit does is to motivate us in the direction of developing our inherent sacred graces.

Some people wonder why administration is listed as a gift of the Holy Spirit. It may seem like a natural talent that anybody might possess—but it isn't. I have no desire and little talent for administration, for example, and neither do many of the men who were called to the priesthood. We had talent for pastoring and preaching and even healing, but not for running a parish and handling money. Administrative duties seemed to take up too large a chunk of my time that I felt would be better spent in prayer, sacred rituals, and spiritual healing services. That's why as a pastor, I always sought out people gifted with administrative ability to do that work.

So we have to do our best to discern what our gifts are and then work to develop them. I sometimes see people, even some prominent teachers, who are called to be healers, but out of fear or some other reason are skirting the issue, and as a result are not being fulfilled in their lives. If I did that, I would feel frustrated, because I can't just teach healing; I have to give healing clinics, because my grace is to teach and to heal. Like most people, I have a number of different graces, but I have to allow the Spirit to lead me by cues to show me where those graces lie, and then I must develop them. The Book of Proverbs says, "It is the glory of God to conceal a thing. It is the glory of man to reveal it." God buries the purpose for our life within us, and our excitement and self-growth lies in discovering and identifying it. If we were issued a handbook at birth listing our life's purpose and telling us exactly how to do it, that would make life pretty boring. It doesn't come to you all at once, and that's part of the fun. Let me use my own life as an example.

Even as a kid, I was a teacher and a leader, directing the games we played in the neighborhood and assigning roles to my playmates. Later I discovered talents as a comedian and actor, and I was also drawn to wrestling and used to love going to professional wrestling matches. I had decided that I wanted to be either a teacher, an actor, or a wrestler—since wrestling and acting clearly have a lot in common! One day I was sitting in the front row at a match featuring Gorgeous George, a wrestler who dressed outrageously and preened before the audience. He was one of the first to understand fully that professional wrestling was more about entertainment than sport, and even Muhammad Ali has acknowledged that he was influenced by George's knack for self-promotion and his dramatic flair. In those early days, the sportswriters sat at ringside with their typewriters, tapping out their stories during the match. At this bout, Gorgeous George threw his opponent out of the ring, and the poor guy landed face first on a typewriter. His face was a bloody mess, and right there I decided against pursuing a career in wrestling.

I couldn't pursue my desire to be an actor because my family didn't have the money to send me to the Pasadena Playhouse, which was where I most wanted to study acting. So by process of elimination, I decided to become a teacher—until I realized that I didn't like the idea of teaching school. Since I loved the scriptures, however, I decided that I would teach the scriptures and pursued a career in ministry. Without question, there is a dramatic side to preaching, and I'm not being sarcastic when I say that many preachers would have made pretty fair actors. Aimee Semple McPherson, the legendary American healer, had a great flair for dramatic presentation, but she applied that talent to her healing work. (The actor Anthony Quinn was a great admirer of McPherson's theatrical grace and expressiveness, and he has said that he based his portrayal of Zorba the Greek—especially the dance that Zorba does in the film—in part on her graceful gestures.)

St. Paul said that each of us must work out our own salvation in fear and trembling, and the Buddha's last words are reported to have been "Work out your salvation with diligence." They were both saying much the same thing: It's up to us to discover our own path. And for that we need the guidance of the Holy Spirit, the "inspirer." A medical doctor specializing in oncology came to me recently complaining that he is getting flak from his hospital because, among other things, he has been an advocate of complementary medicine—combining naturopathic and homeopathic healing with the allopathic kind embraced by the American Medical Association. He talked incessantly about starting his own clinic but insisted that he couldn't take the chance of leaving the hospital because his family needed the security of a steady income. It was plain to see that he needed to go out on his own and follow his heart, yet he couldn't bring himself to make that decision. He was afraid to rely on his intuition and reinvent his life's work. God's plan is for us to reinvent ourselves and our work constantly as we go along. The Sufi mystic Ibn Arabi said that God creates the universe anew in each moment, and I think He expects us to imitate Him as much as possible.

The desire for financial security is a flimsy excuse for not following your intuition. I like the parable of the man who goes on a journey and gives his servants each a different number of *talents* (Matt. 25:14-30). The talent was a Hebrew measure of weight used for gold and silver and represented a considerable sum of money. The meaning of our word *talent* as a divine endowment of ability actually derives from its use in that parable. Two of the servants invest the talents their master gives them, and they increase their wealth. "Well done, good and faithful servant," the master tells them. "You have been faithful over a little; I will set you over much. Enter into the joy of your master." The third servant, however, buries his talent in the ground for fear of losing it. At first blush, one might think that a wise course because he didn't risk his master's money—but he is the only one who incurs his master's wrath for his fearful attitude. Many of us today are not prosperous because we're not uncovering all of our gifts.

Resting in the Spirit

One of the gifts most commonly misunderstood is an experience called "resting in the Spirit," or "going down under the power." If you've ever witnessed one of those TV revival meetings with some glossy-haired preacher in a thousand-dollar suit, you may have seen him walking along a row of people, touching each one on the forehead and standing back as they crumple into the arms of his assistants, known as "catchers." All of this is accompanied by loud, boisterous music programmed to evoke powerful emotions in the congregation and the viewing audience. That's the circus version of resting in the Spirit, and a skeptical observer might assume that either the preacher is pushing them down or the members are merely responding in a choreographed fashion to what amounts to little more than an empty ritual. Yet, I have also observed and been a part of the real thing, and the real thing can be powerful indeed.

Although nobody fully understands the phenomenon of resting in the Spirit, I have observed over the last 20 years that when people need deep inner healing on some unconscious level, they may genuinely go down under the power while God heals their wounds directly. I have been told by people who have carried guilt from acts committed years ago that the greatest healers in the world have laid hands on them and nothing happened. But when they went down under the power and got up, they felt like a new person. Often there is nothing that a counselor or psychologist or even a minister or priest can do for you, but the Spirit of God *can*.

During this process, God's divine essence seems to take hold at a deep level to clear out whatever is blocking the healing process. Usually this is because something within those people is too painful to face consciously, and so God in His mercy takes care of it in an unconscious fashion. It is as if the supernatural power of the Holy Spirit passing through a body short-circuits all the body's functions for a moment. Muscles and nerves that are usually controlled by electrical currents from the brain are overpowered or bypassed—as if a million volts of lightning were to strike the electrical system of a house that is wired for 220 volts. In such a case, the power would leap all relays and fuses, making every appliance inoperative. In much the same way, the power of the Holy Spirit flooding through a human body can cause the person to collapse to the floor. Unlike lightning striking a home, however, resting in the Spirit causes not harm, but deep healing.

In these cases, the ailment or disability is generally connected to some traumatic memory that is too painful to be processed on a conscious level. It could be a memory of childhood abuse or a traumatic injury or other event such as the loss of a parent or sibling. Following the healing that often results from resting in the Spirit, at a future time when the sting of traumatic pain no longer accompanies the memory, the person will be able to recall it consciously. The great healer Agnes Sanford called this the "healing of memories," but that term was misinterpreted because people thought that she meant when the bad memory was healed they wouldn't have it anymore. In fact, they will still have the memory, but the pain associated with it—the headaches and stomach upsets and emotional and psychological torment—will no longer accompany the memory.

Recent scientific studies have shown that as much as 80 percent of our ailments and disabilities are caused by various forms of mental and emotional stress. Jesus already knew this, which is why he was always telling people not to fear or worry. So, too, did the Buddha, more than 2,500 years ago, when he encouraged his followers not to regret the past or dread the future, but to live in the eternal present. The 20th-century Indian master Meher Baba was famous for his simple saying, "Don't worry. Be happy." Despite all their teachings, however, we continue to let ourselves be overcome by regret, dread, worry, and anxiety, all of which contribute to stress and bad health. We further stress our bodies by eating improperly, drinking too much, smoking, engaging in high-risk sexual activity, and even by polluting the environment. When you add those physical stressors to psychological and emotional ones, it's no wonder that we are in the midst of an epidemic of chronic fatigue and depression.

Given all that stress and the unconscious traumatic memories that many of us carry, resting in the Spirit can be an invaluable healing modality. Merely falling to the floor when one is touched by the healer, however, does not signify the authenticity of the act. I know people who have claimed on numerous occasions to have gone down under the power, and they looked more miserable when they got up than when they went down. That is not the power of God; that is their own "power." One man came to my healing services quite often, and once after going down, he got up and gleefully announced, "This is the 25th time I've gone down under the power!" Yet it was never reflected in his life or even in his face.

If your face does not radiate more peace, security, confidence, or self-esteem, then I doubt it is the power of God. I have often seen people fake receiving the gifts of the Spirit. They look first to see if there is a catcher behind them before they go down. One woman actually took out her handkerchief and dusted off the spot on the floor before she fell onto it. Jesus clearly says, "By their fruit you shall know them." I always tell people not to get excited when they see someone go down, but to get excited when they come up happier than they were. Be excited when you see the peace of God all over their faces. Get excited when you sense a new self-worth pouring through them.

On the other side of the ledger, I have sometimes witnessed people who have not even been touched, yet have gone down under the power and come up healed and have set aside their canes and crutches. There have been moments in my healing services when my assistants and I have laid hands on people, and you could hear the crackle of electricity in their bodies. I have had the experience of placing my hands on people and feeling the electric charge as they jumped into the air, feet sticking straight out, and then went down on their backs. Those have been awesome nights.

I often think that's the way God wakes up some people. One night when 20 or 30 people were falling at one time, the assistants who serve as catchers just threw up their hands as if to say, "Oh, what's the use?" One older woman fell down on her side, her glasses flew off, and it sounded as if her head cracked. I thought, *Oh, dear Lord, I hope she didn't go down by herself.* The next day she came to a prayer service, and I asked her how she was feeling.

"You know," she said, "that's the way God had to do it to get my attention."

When I asked what she meant, she said, "I always went around saying, 'Oh, I do believe.' And I always followed that with 'but.' 'I do believe, but. . . . I trust God, but. . . .' After last night, I'll never say 'but' again."

She went on to describe what had happened to her. "It was like a hand came and pushed me and knocked me to the floor. And yet I don't hurt, and I don't have any pain."

Feeling the Power

In the early 1980s, I became acquainted with John Wimber, a teacher and healer who began his career by arranging songs for the Righteous Brothers and went on to write best-selling books such as *Power Evangelism* and *Power Points.* He also founded the Vineyard Christian Fellowship in California, which grew from a home prayer meeting to hundreds of congregations around the world. What impressed me most about Wimber was his belief that you cannot have effective spiritual ministry if you don't also attend to people's corporal needs, such as feeding the hungry. He had an enormous warehouse full of food that his congregation collected and distributed to hungry folks. John and I became good friends before he died, and one day when we were sitting and talking, he mentioned a passage in the Gospel of John (18:4-6) that he felt made no impact in any of the available translations. The scene is the garden of Gethsemane, when Judas leads the soldiers and officers from the chief priests and Pharisees to arrest Jesus and bring him to trial. Knowing all that is going to happen to him, Jesus goes out to meet them and asks them, "Who is it you want?" They reply that they seek Jesus of Nazareth, and he answers, "I am he."

When Jesus said that, the scripture reads, "They drew back and fell to the ground." Wimber insisted that this is a poor translation, because the original Greek actually means, "They were knocked back and propelled to the ground." Jesus had such a connection with the eternal "I AM" of the heavenly Father/Mother that when that vibration went out, it connected with the energy in the soldiers' bodies and stupefied them. Whether they all fell into a dead faint is not the point. The real significance of that passage properly translated is that the power that emanated from Jesus is available to anyone who truly knows the I AM.

The Greek text also states that Judas brought with him a "cohort" from the royal garrison to arrest Jesus. A cohort was one of ten divisions of a Roman legion, and at that time would have been 500 to 600 soldiers. Yet according to the text, all of them went down when Jesus acknowledged "I am he." That's a lot of power! The Bible is full of such unexplained events that seem almost taken for granted unless you consider that at the time they were written, most people probably knew exactly what the authors were talking about. Wimber made the point that this and other accounts in the scriptures referred to as "signs and wonders" ought to be occurring today, especially among the followers of Jesus. If, as Jesus said, "All this and more shall you do if you have faith," why aren't we using spiritual power in the same way Jesus did? We need to connect with that power, which is the power of the Holy Spirit, the manifestation of God's energy on earth. I believe this to be true for all people, including those on spiritual paths other than Christianity. That's where prayer, faith, confidence, and self-esteem come in.

The passages to which Wimber was referring all deal with people being struck by powerful energies of some sort. For instance, in Acts 9:3-9, Paul is knocked to the ground by a light; he hears the voice of the Lord and is temporarily blinded. In the next chapter of Acts (10:9-10), Peter goes up to the roof of a house to pray and falls into a trance, during which he sees a vision of "all kinds of animals and reptiles and birds of the air," which a voice tells him to kill and eat. Peter says he can't eat all of them because some are "common or unclean," but the voice replies, "What God has cleansed, you must not call common." This seems to be an indication that Peter will universalize the new tradition, removing it from the dietary and social restrictions of Judaism.

In the Gospel of Matthew 28:1-4, an angel of the Lord rolls away the stone from the crypt where Jesus was buried "and the soldiers fell into a dead faint." In Genesis 2:21, Adam is put into a deep sleep. In Revelations 1:17, the narrator has an ecstatic vision of "one like a son of man" whose "face was like the sun shining with all its force. When I saw him I fell at his feet as though I were dead." And Daniel 10:10 says, "A hand touched me and knocked me to my knees." These are all examples of what can happen when the power of God's Holy Spirit is released.

Keep in mind that all these events took place around prayer in some form or other: Jesus had been praying in the garden. Peter was praying on the rooftop. Paul hadn't been praying, but he went into prayer after he was knocked to the ground and had a life-changing experience. Daniel had been praying and fasting for three weeks before the vision came that forced him to his knees. In these events, the subjects received a personal experience that God *Is*. They needed these experiences just as we do. Churches that deny these experiences are denying their congregations the opportunity to feel hope. We need miracles now more than ever before. We need the personal experience of signs and wonders to give us hope again.

When people go down under the power at a healing service, however, their loved ones often cry out fearfully, wondering what has happened. I sometimes have to tell them to leave the person alone. Once in Chicago, a young woman who had never been to a service before fell down as I walked past her. I don't stop to pick up people who have gone down because it's best for them to get up in their own time, when they're ready. As I walked past this girl on my way back, however, the Lord said, "Pick her up." Approaching her, I noticed her mother lightly tapping her face as if to snap her out of it. I said, "Sit down and leave her alone." People get excited at times and you have to be very firm with them. I knelt down and spoke to the young woman—I don't even remember what I said, but as she looked at me and wiped away the tears, I told her to stand up. When she took me by the hand and got up, her mother started crying, but I couldn't understand what was wrong. Not until afterwards did I learn from the team members that her daughter had arthritis throughout her entire body and should not have been able to get up at all. She had been in constant pain, but from that moment on, she experienced complete relief.

Resting in the Spirit is not to be confused with a state known as "being drunk in the Spirit," the kind of divine inebriation described in Jeremiah, to which I referred earlier. When people are drunk in the Spirit, they often become giddy, just as if they'd had too much wine. This has sometimes happened at my healing services, and when the people go back to their seats, they typically are trying to hold their mouths or are laughing out loud. I have subsequently found out that sometimes these people haven't laughed in years and are known as neighborhood curmudgeons. God is touching them, and that's a healing.

As seductive as these gifts of the Spirit can be, Paul himself makes a significant distinction between the gifts and the fruit of the Spirit that becomes clear in the Amplified Bible's expanded translation: "But earnestly desire and zealously cultivate the higher (gifts) and the choicest (graces), and yet I will show you a still more excellent way—one that is better by far and the highest of them all (love)." The highest form of love, as I am certain Paul understands it, is God's love, which is unconditional. God loves us not for what we *do* but simply because we *are*. Unfortunately, unconditional love does not come easily to us, and perhaps a large part of why we are here on earth in the first place is to learn how to demonstrate it in our daily life.

Exercise: "I Am Love"

Since expressing unconditional love for others goes against everything most of us have been taught, we'll need to pay special attention to learning how. One exercise that has helped me greatly has been to work with the following lines from Paul's First Letter to the Corinthians, 13:4-8a, part of his famous disquisition on love:

Love is patient and kind; love is not jealous or boastful; it is not arrogant or rude. Love does not insist on its own way; it is not irritable or resentful; it does not rejoice at wrong, but rejoices in the right. Love bears all things, believes all things, hopes all things, endures all things. Love never ends. . . .

I generally begin by reading that passage and then rereading it, but substituting the name of God for the word *love:*

God is patient and kind; God is not jealous or boastful; He is not arrogant or rude . . . and so on.

Then comes the challenging part: Wherever the word *love* appears in that passage, I substitute my own name:

Ron is patient and kind; Ron is not jealous or boastful; he is not arrogant or rude. . . .

By the time I get to "Ron does not insist on his own way," I've really stretched the limits of my tolerance! But saying it in the third person somehow makes it a little easier for me to believe in the truth of what I'm saying regarding who I really am. Even if you don't quite believe that you are not irritable or resentful, or that you bear all things, believe all things, hope all things, and endure all things, say the words as if you do. Buddhist teachers often speak of realizing that we are already fully enlightened Buddhas—it's just that we don't realize it yet. So don't worry about your belief level as you do this exercise. Say the words in good faith, trusting that the Holy Spirit will help you to realize their truth over time.

Tapping the Healing Power of Unconditional Love

Many meditative traditions that were developed in the East, including those modified and presented in this country by American masters, have fairly rigid rules and guidelines for practice. One rule that I have come across frequently is that meditation is a time for doing nothing, and that you should let nothing interrupt you during this practice. The idea is that when you let all the surface nattering of your mind die down by sitting still in a quiet spot and focusing on your breathing, then deeper, more creative thoughts may surface. Most meditation masters don't want you to get caught up in those thoughts, and they generally advise you not to interrupt your meditation to write down ideas or hunches that occur to you in this relaxed state. That approach may have worked well in the

8th century, or the 18th, but it doesn't have much to do with living the spiritual life in the practical world today. I believe that the Holy Spirit is my helper, and one of the times Spirit can come through to me most forcibly is when my mind is clear. So I can only assume that whatever little voices or inklings of ideas I'm hearing during prayer or meditation are coming from God—and why wouldn't I want to make a record of that?

To this end, I try to keep a notepad or blank paper nearby during my spiritual practice time for the very purpose of availing myself of any inspiration that flows through me then. If I make an effort not to write things down, I'll either forget them altogether or I'll try so hard to remember them without writing them down that I'll distract myself even more. Instead, writing down these thoughts and hunches frees me to continue my prayer or meditation without dwelling on them.

EXERCISE: VISUALIZING THE CHRIST

The world is awash in images of Jesus, many of them of a blond-haired man with a neatly combed beard, despite the fact that as a Jew of that time and place, he probably had dark hair and a dark complexion. Some of these images of Jesus make him look pasty and foolish. A few are more appealing, among them Rembrandt's 17th-century painting *Head of Jesus,* which shows a swarthy, Semitic-looking Jesus with deeply compassionate eyes. You are free to visualize the Christ Presence however you like. He is the energy of love and forgiveness in human form. At a certain point in my own spiritual evolution, I had to stop seeing Jesus as merely a religious figure and begin to see him as the most practical, dynamic motivator who ever lived. When I look at Jesus, I want to see that practical side, filled with joy and peace, and I want to hear a teaching that will tell me how to move through life. I've always found the great Christian mystics such as Ignatius Loyola and Teresa of Avila to be eminently practical. Their work wasn't about knowing God in some absolute or abstract way, but about knowing God in this world. And one way to know God in this world is to experience Him as unconditional love, because that is also who you are and who you were meant to be—unconditional love.

Above all, we need forgiveness. Without its kindly light, we grope in darkness, using reason to justify our rage and our attacks. Our understanding is so limited that what we think we understand is but confusion born of error. The only ones who can be born again are those who have forgiven everyone else. Your function on earth is simply to forgive. Forgive everyone's sins this moment and you will see that you are one with those you forgive, with God, and with yourself. Forgive and be forgiven. Say to yourself or out loud now:

I am the light of the world.
I have come to forgive.
I have come to be love.
There is nothing to fear.
I belong to God.
God is in me.
I am at peace.
I am the light of the world.
My major function in life is to forgive.

During this exercise in visualizing the Christ energy in human form, Jesus is going to touch you and reveal to you who you really are.

I want you to imagine Jesus standing in front of you. You can picture him any way you like—dressed in medieval robes as he has been depicted in thousands of paintings; wearing the simple, ancient garb of Judea in his day; or casually attired in blue jeans and sneakers with dark, curly hair. Now I want you to imagine that Jesus is holding your face in his hands; your eyes are looking into his eyes, and his eyes are looking deeply into yours. Can you feel the warm hands of Jesus on your face? The two of you are going to become one, and you are going to sense that you are where you are supposed to be and you are who you are supposed to be—unconditional love.

As you look into Jesus' eyes and let him look into yours, you begin to sense what unconditional love is really all about, and somehow you know that you have to be this love to others. The Spirit of God within you is saying that unconditional love liberates by communicating to loved ones that they can be whoever they are, and that they can express all their thoughts, feelings, and desires with absolute confidence. They will not be punished for their openness and honesty.

Now I want you to see a garbage can in front of you. Take all of those hurts that you have had within you and throw them into the garbage can. Jesus is standing on the other side of that garbage can smiling at you, and after you fill that garbage can with all your painful and negative experiences, he puts a lid on it. He is tying beautiful colored balloons to it. Now the balloons are rising up from the ground, carrying that garbage can with its burden of pain and hurt into the air heading toward the sun, farther and farther away from you. Finally, it is all gone. You never need to live that way again, filled with fears and doubts and confusion. Jesus has taken away all of that. Unconditional love heals. It stimulates our growth toward the kind of self-acceptance God means us to have.

As you rest in the peace of knowing that you are unconditional love, take a moment to meditate on the nature of that love. It is so unfamiliar to most of us that when Jesus wanted to explain it to the people of his day, he told them the story of the Good Samaritan. That story is well known even to non-Christians, and yet in reading and studying it over and over again, I began to be overwhelmed by what it was teaching me. At the same time, I felt unable to formulate those insights into words to pass on to others. So one day in prayer I just said, "Lord, this story is revealing so much to me about myself and about what we are called to be that I can't take it all in. How do I sum it up? How can I teach all of these principles and ideas?" Then there came to me 14 points about unconditional love, the love that God has called us to have by being connected with Him, with ourselves, and with each other.

1. Unconditional love does not have to agree with the choice of the beloved, but offers you the chance to grow, expand your horizons, and become full. It offers understanding, kindness, and encouragement. If you want to see changes in your families, this is what you have to practice.

2. Unconditional love liberates by communicating to the beloved that you can be whoever you are with the absolute confidence that God will not punish you

for your openness and honesty. You are free to be yourself and to express all your thoughts, feelings, and desires.

3. Unconditional love says, "I will not reject you even if I disagree with you. I will always love you even if you don't do things my way." This frees you as well as the one you love to grow and become. Inner healing is a process of becoming a new person.

4. Unconditional love shatters the delusion that criticism, punishment, and even correction given negatively stimulate a person to grow.

5. Unconditional love does not lay guilt trips on the loved one. If you are having trouble with excessive guilt, don't think that God is doing that to you. These kinds of guilt feelings are probably the residue of childhood traumas, scoldings, and overly harsh and demeaning corrections. God may speak to us about times when we have been unkind or

lacked compassion, but that is more like being taken aside by a kindly grandfather who sits you on his knee and gently but firmly explains something you've done that needs to be corrected.

6. Unconditional love does not attempt to manipulate or coerce to get what it wants, nor does it give rewards to others for being what someone else wants them to be. Instilling fear is manipulative.

7. Unconditional loves implies open and honest relationships as well as vital and real conversation. Many times we like to think that we are communicating, but we are actually talking about ideas or about other people rather than communicating feelings.

8. Unconditional love is the courage to share our deepest thoughts and feelings. It is aware that loved ones have no x-ray vision that allows them to know what we are thinking and feeling. I'm sensitive to feelings that people

emanate, but I don't read minds. Even my closest friends have to tell me what their preferences are.

9. Unconditional love does not allow one party to use another, which would be harmful to both parties.

10. Unconditional love does not automatically do things for others that they can do for themselves. In Dr. Jerry Jampolsky's original Center for Attitudinal Healing in California, children who were suffering from catastrophic illnesses such as cancer set up a national phone line that allowed other kids their age or a little younger to call them and talk, not to the staff, but to the children themselves. The children helped each other, teaching love, because that's what they are. But the staff would not do for them what they could and should do for themselves. Anything else makes people feel helpless by fostering a self-image of worthlessness.

11. Unconditional love offers both a sense of belonging and a sense of independence and freedom. We are hardest on others in areas about which we feel guilty ourselves. When you find yourself obsessing about a particular weakness in someone you know, try turning your attention to yourself. See others as teachers who are helping you by reflecting what you don't like about yourself.

12. Unconditional love invites the beloved to stretch, to grow beyond old limitations, to attempt what was always considered too difficult, to break a self-destructive habit, to rise above fear, to give up a grudge, to open a repressed feeling, to confront a difficult situation, or to offer a painful apology. Although you don't condone what others may be doing, you still cannot condemn them, or you condemn yourself to the same fate. Read any psychology book or any case history. If you've condemned your father for being an alcoholic, it's likely that you fear becoming one yourself.

If you have condemned your mother because she was unable to sustain a romantic relationship, you may be expressing unconscious disapproval of your own conduct. You need to reach out to love and help, not condemn or judge. Even our pulpits are used for un-Christlike judging, when they should be used for reaching out; the church is not a museum for saints, but a hospital for people who need healing.

Keep in mind that what you focus on, you become. If you are always focused on the negative aspects of others' conduct, you may generate that conduct in yourself. I call this the Jimmy Swaggart syndrome. Rather than focusing on negative judgments, I prefer to follow Paul's advice in Phillippians 4:8: "Let your minds be filled with everything that is true, everything that is honorable, everything that is upright and pure, everything that we love and admire—with whatever is good and praiseworthy." In Romans 12:2, Paul adds, "Do not model your behavior on the contemporary world, but let the renewing of your minds transform you, so that you may discern for yourselves the will of God—what is good and acceptable and mature." In other words, look upward for your inspiration by focusing on positive qualities, not on what you see wrong in everybody else. It sounds obvious, but it's not easy to do.

13. Unconditional love says to the beloved, "Do it! Go ahead and stretch. If you succeed, I'll be right there in the front row applauding and cheering the loudest. But if you fail, I'll still be sitting there next to you. I'll hold on to you. We are in this together."

14. Unconditional love heals and stimulates our growth toward the kind of self-acceptance God means us to have. Anyone who embarks on a spiritual path without love has lost heart, and as far as God is concerned, has lost everything. The healing power of God flows

> when we love people and reach out to them—not because of what we can get, but because of what we can give—and in that giving we receive.

You may think that one of the 14 points I've just outlined ought to take you a day or two to understand and master. But I suggest that you spend at least a month on each one. Concentrate on working with each of the points in depth until you understand it fully, rather than zipping through them in a mechanical fashion. You may find that they unfold gradually, until each one reveals the kernel of wisdom at its heart. Only then is it time to move on to the next point. Every day as you perform the exercise described at the beginning of this section, dwell for a time on the point that you intend to work with that day. This will help you remind yourself where to place your focus.

Starting Your Own Prayer Group to Release the Power of the Holy Spirit

While I was a pastor at a small rural parish, some of my parishioners approached me to start a Bible study group in addition to the much larger prayer community that already met one night a week. Although they had, for the most part, never attended a Bible study or prayer meeting until recently, they felt a need to seek God and find Him in the sacred scriptures and through prayer, just as members of the early Christian church did on a more personal level, as recorded in the Book of Acts: "They met constantly to hear the

Apostles teach, to share the common life, to break bread (communion) and to pray." (2:42, New English Bible)

I structured this particular fellowship group to create a vehicle by which the Holy Spirit could operate through them as She operates through me, whether on the level of five people or 5,000. This same structure can serve as a guideline for your group, wherever it meets and however many members it comprises. As you remain open to the Spirit's prompting, you will feel increasingly free to expand within this particular structure in the way God wants you to. What I am presenting here is only a brief outline and not a method or structure that must be followed to the letter to be effective. God is the one who makes our work effective. We cooperate with Him or Her (if you prefer, use the feminine pronouns when you are referring to God in your prayer group, since God is both Father and Mother). But God is the one who directs our efforts and brings them to fruition. As it says in the Book of Proverbs 3:6, "In everything you do, put God first, and He will direct you and crown you with success." By doing your part, give God an opportunity to show Himself to you as He promised.

Begin by having the following scriptures read aloud, either by the facilitator or by each of the members in turn until they have all been read. You should also feel free to substitute quotations of your own from any of the sacred writings of the world that you find appropriate:

"But you will also begin to search again for Jehovah your God, and you shall find Him when you search for Him with all your heart and soul." (Deuteronomy 4:29)

"For I know the plans I have for you, says the Lord. They are plans for good and not for evil, to give you a future and a hope. In those days when you pray, I will listen. You will find me when you seek me, if you look for me in earnest." (Jeremiah 29:11-13)

"O you who believe! If you help God's cause, He will help you and will make your foothold firm." (Quran 47:7)

"Ask me and I will tell you remarkable secrets which you have never known before." (Jeremiah 33:3)

"United with me, you shall overcome all difficulties by my grace." (Bhagavad Gita 18:58)

"He fulfills the desires of those who reverence and trust Him: He hears their cries for help and rescues them." (Psalms 145:19)

"Open yourself to the Tao, then trust your natural responses; and everything will fall into place." (Tao Te Ching 23)

Preparation by Group Facilitators

Remembering that the fruits of the Spirit include peace, harmony, and tranquility (Gal. 5:22), as well as decent order (I Cor. 14), be sure the meeting place is conducive to a spirit of quietness, healing, and meditation. Distractions make it almost impossible to concentrate on prayer and to listen to God and one another. Prior to gathering together, each facilitator ought to do the following:

1. Individually pray, asking God to touch every person who is coming to the

meeting in a very special way and to give wisdom and an outpouring of the Spirit during the meeting.

2. Arrange chairs in an informal circle. I find that it helps people focus their thoughts on the Word of God and Its transforming power to have an open "Bible" of any religious tradition—the Hebrew Bible, New Testament, Upanishads, Dhammapada, Tao Te Ching, or Quran—along with sacred images, whether of Jesus, one of the saints (including modern holy people such as Mother Teresa or Padre Pio), Indian or Buddhist masters of present or past, a crucifix, the Star of David, Arabic calligraphy or any other spiritual emblem, or candles on a table. Little aids such as these can be very helpful for concentrating, centering one's thoughts, quieting one's inner self, and going into meditation.

3. If refreshments are to be served after the meeting, it is best that they not be in the

same area where people are praying, as the sight or smell of them may become a distraction to prayer. As a matter of policy, refreshments should *never* be available before the meeting, as they may distract those who want to prepare themselves in quietness. I personally discourage offering anything but water as a refreshment, because anything more tends to place too big a burden on the host and is not necessary for prayer. Members can always go out for coffee afterwards if they so desire.

4. It is very helpful to discourage smoking, either before or after the meeting, as smoke itself tends to irritate many people's eyes, throats, or breathing. Former smokers may find the smell of tobacco smoke especially disturbing. If you are a smoker, you might consider, as an act of love, to begin practicing discipline in this area of your life, especially if the group is meeting in a small enclosure. Needless to say, I do not expect everyone to give up smoking

immediately, but we have a right to expect everyone to begin practicing care and concern for others as a manifestation of true Love. This act of self-discipline might be offered to God as a "fast," seeking His blessings on the meeting.

5. At the onset, it is wise to have name tags for each person until you get to know one another on a first-name basis. As new people are led into your fellowship, please be considerate of their needs, fears, and anxieties; and make them feel wanted, loved, and cared for. If your group is small enough, have everyone introduce themselves to the newcomers and welcome them. If it is a larger group, you might wish to have someone at the doorway greeting people and "spotting" newcomers, presenting them with any information concerning the meeting that they may read as they prepare for this spiritual encounter. Remember, as a spiritual community, it is imperative that you be

friendly to all. Be careful of cliquishness, socializing with the same few, and ignoring others. If this happens, chances are that your group will die rather quickly. Use common sense. Remember when people are coming to pray, and be there to greet them. This is not the time to be off somewhere in a back room "praying." Your personal prayer should already be completed before people begin to arrive. A physical fitness instructor does not spend time working out while members are walking into the room, and neither should a spiritual fitness facilitator.

"Be compassionate (all inclusive) as God is compassionate (all inclusive). People will know you are my disciples by the love you have for one another." (Jesus of Nazareth)

"Those who act kindly in this world will have kindness." (Quran 39:10)

"Those who pray for their neighbors, while they themselves have the same needs, will be answered first." (Talmud, Baba Kamma 92a)

6. Discuss briefly the format of this fellowship gathering and its purpose—to pray and grow in the Spirit of God. Encourage everyone to contribute their input and talents to build the body in faith, love, peace, joy, and maturity. After everyone seems settled, be prepared to enter into prayer.

Prayer Structure of the Group

I. Opening prayer and scripture reading

This basic structure is also adaptable for larger prayer gatherings, such as prayer meetings in an auditorium. The opening prayer is followed by readings from various sacred scriptures of your choice, but dealing with some aspect of God's goodness, joy, love, healing, and so forth. For example: *"I am convinced that nothing can ever separate us from His love. Death can't and life can't. The angels won't and all the powers of hell itself cannot keep God's love away. Our fears for today, our worries about tomorrow or where we are—high above the sky or in the deepest oceans—nothing will ever be able to separate us from the love of God demonstrated by Jesus."* (Romans 8:37-39)

This scripture passage can, by its nature, lead into:

II. Worship, praise, songs and/or words of thanksgiving

This segment consists of singing simple songs, praying spontaneously and informally. For example, "Thank you, God, for _______________. Heavenly Father-Mother, I worship you who are God Almighty, Creator of the earth and all that is in it." Or share a Psalm or a personal prayer of gratitude, worship, adoration (examples: Psalm 8, 96, 100, 103, 104, 150), or even a favorite poem or song lyric if it moves your heart. Being aware of God's goodness and love leads to a humble, grateful heart. Thus, we enter into a spirit of:

III. Confession, repentance, cleansing of self

"Don't drink too much wine, for many evils lie along that path; be filled instead with the Holy Spirit and controlled by Her. Talk with each other much about

the Lord, quoting psalms and hymns and singing sacred songs, making music in your hearts to the Lord. Always give thanks for everything to our God." (Ephesians 5:18-20)

Choose one or more Psalms from Psalm 32 through Psalm 51, all of which are Psalms of inner healing, and let the facilitator read slowly and meditatively while the others take it in. Instrumental music may be played softly in the background while the Psalms are read. Follow whatever physical actions or postures the Spirit leads you to do during this time. For example, if you are prompted toward humility and patience, you may feel guided to kneel or lie prostrate on the floor. After the reading of the Psalms, there should be a quiet time of individual introspection for about 15 to 20 minutes. A guided meditation by the group facilitator can also be introduced here, if you choose.

The Examen: Time to review one's actions in the light of love without judgment or condemnation (led by the facilitator in the context of cleansing oneself).

The ancient mystical practice of daily self-examination known as the *examen* takes its name from the Latin word for the tongue of a balance used in Rome for weighing gold. In the Roman Catholic tradition, this practice has been reduced to a rather demeaning "examination of conscience" preceding the sacrament of Penance, during which one is supposed to remember one's sins in excruciating detail. The self-flagellation implicit in this approach probably outweighs any benefit. What I am talking about is less judgmental but more demanding than that. Here are some sample questions you might ask yourself. Bear in mind that they are only suggestions; over time, you can improvise your own questions.

A. Love of God

- Is God the most important person in my life?
- Do I consider His will in all of my decisions? Or do I think only of myself?
- Do I respect the Names of God and honor them and all that they represent?

- Do I honestly try to develop my relationship with the Divine?
- Have I learned to trust God's direction for me?
- Do I worship God daily in times of prayer and meditation?

B. Love of Self

- Have I discovered who I am?
- Am I trying to improve myself spiritually?
- Do I lead a balanced life with adequate rest, exercise, and proper diet?
- Am I free to admit that I sometimes make mistakes or could use the help of others?
- Do I ask for forgiveness or for help?
- Am I satisfied with the direction my life is going?
- Do I allow love or fear to guide me?

C. Love of Neighbor

- Do I treat others in the way I would have them treat me?
- Do I share myself in an open, honest communication with those I love?
- Do I allow others the freedom to lead their own lives and still accept them?
- Do I offer loving support to others (both physical and emotional)?
- Or do I criticize others and waste the good things I could share with them?

A spirit of humble awareness during the examen will lead one to:

IV. Quietness before the Lord

A two-way prayer (contemplation) during which God speaks to us.

"Be still and know I am God." (Psalm 46:10)

"You cannot mirror yourself in running water—you can mirror yourself only in still

water. Only that which is still can still the stillness of other things." (Chuang Tzu 5)

"'Go out and stand before me on the mountain,' the Lord told him. And as Elijah stood there the Lord passed by, and a mighty windstorm hit the mountain; it was such a terrible blast that the rocks were torn loose, but the Lord was not in the wind. After the wind, an earthquake, but the Lord was not in the earthquake; and after the earthquake a fire, but the Lord was not in the fire. And after the fire, the sound of a gentle whisper [a still small voice]. When Elijah heard it, he wrapped his face in his scarf and went out and stood at the entrance of the cave. And a voice said, 'Why are you here, Elijah?'" (1 Kings 19:11-13)

"Just as a deep lake is clear and still, even so, on hearing the teachings and realizing them, the wise become exceedingly peaceful." (Dhammapada 82)

"Worship me through meditation in the sanctuary of the heart." (Bhagavata Purana 11:5)

After one encounters God in the silence, one is usually desirous of a quiet time with soft music to listen to God and maybe take "notes" as to what one is "hearing." Facilitators might remind members to bring notebooks and pens for this purpose.

Manifestations of spiritual graces may occur at this time. For an understanding of this phenomenon, refer back to the section of this book entitled "The Gifts and the Fruit of the Holy Spirit," on page 67.

> *"Well, then, my brothers and sisters, whenever you meet, let every one be ready to contribute a psalm, a teaching, a spiritual truth, or a song of praise. Everything should be done to make you strong in your faith."* (1 Cor. 14:28)

Spiritual teaching may be given by the facilitator and/or either audio- or videocassettes from any worthwhile spiritual teacher. Those groups that are ready to move to in-depth weekly teaching but feel that they are not qualified to teach the sacred scriptures can purchase any of my sets of teaching tapes dealing with spiritual subjects. Each week, prepare yourself by studying segments of the scriptures contained in the lessons, and then listen to the tapes at the meeting. Follow this by sharing with each other ways in which one can apply the principles found in the tapes to one's personal daily life. Allow the Holy Spirit time to work in you. Don't rush. Absorb the teachings, and let them become a part of you. Pray for wisdom and enlightenment.

> *"At 15, I set my heart upon learning.*
> *At 30, I had planted my feet upon firm ground.*
> *At 40, I no longer suffered from perplexities.*
> *At 50, I knew what were the biddings of heaven.*
> *At 60, I heard them with a docile ear.*
> *At 70, I could follow the dictates of my own heart, for what I desired no longer overstepped the boundaries of right."* (Confucius, Analects 2:4)

Miracle Prayer Circles

All participants break into small groups of two or three (or more if you have a large number) and take turns praying for each other. You don't need to take a lot of time specifying each other's needs. You can simply hold hands and allow the facilitator to offer prayers for the benefit of all. As individual members feel comfortable with this, they can allow prayers to come forth from them in turn.

V. Supplication, intercessory prayer, healing prayer, and concluding praise

Intercession (see examples in the Appendix dealing with Intercessory Prayer. For a more detailed explanation of intercessory prayer, see my book *The Healing Path of Prayer,* pp. 35–36).

VI. Personal ministry time and laying on of hands by the facilitator

A special note: Please do not be discouraged by your first attempts to be a spiritual community. Give the Holy Spirit time to operate in each individual as well as your group as a whole. Soon you will begin to experience Her power, healing love, peace, and joy at work in you and among you. There will be an excitement and an enthusiasm springing up within you as you anticipate each "meeting" as an encounter with the Divine as well as an encounter with loved ones who share a common bond with you and God.

"They worshiped together regularly at the Temple each day, met in small groups in homes

for Communion, and shared their meals with great joy and thankfulness praising God." (Acts 2:46-47, Living Bible)

"Those who, knowing my true nature, worship me steadfastly are my true devotees. Worship me in the symbols and images which remind you of me, and also in the hearts of my devotees, where I am most manifest. . . . Observe the forms and rituals set forth in the scriptures, without losing sight of their inner spirit." (Bhagavata Purana 11:5)

"They continued steadily learning the teaching of the apostles and joined in their fellowship in the breaking of bread and in prayer." (Acts 2:42, Phillips Bible)

"Let us do it
The way it is usually done
So that we may have the usual result."
(Yoruba proverb)

"Of all the prayers of the heart, the best prayer is the prayer to the Master to be given the grace of properly praising the Lord." (Adi Granth)

For an added dimension of prayer and fuller involvement in the life of the Spirit, you might also wish to consider a celebration of the Breaking of Bread. See Chapter 9, "New Sacraments in Daily Rituals," in *The Healing Path of Prayer,* concerning personal use of the Sacraments.

If you choose to, on special occasions you may ask everyone to bring a covered dish for a fellowship dinner following the time of prayer. Each one is able to manifest love in yet another dimension on the practical level by preparing a dish in which other brothers and sisters will have an opportunity to share. The early mystical communities were a brotherhood and sisterhood, bound together by God's love for them and their love of God, manifested by their love for one another.

> *"And day by day the Lord added to their number those whom He was healing."* (Acts 2:47b)

Remember, there is no shortcut to growth. Give God your best, and be open for God's best. My aim for your group is that you become more aware of your Divine Essence in order to live, move, and have your being in the Holy Spirit. The fruits of these meetings begin to show themselves in your daily dealings with others, through acts of love and service. In the words of Padre Pio, "If your prayer does not lead to love, it is not prayer."

God Loves You, and So Do I!

Appendix

The following prayer, adapted from Ephesians 1:16ff, can be said for yourself or others by changing the pronouns from first to third person.

I do not cease to give thanks to God, my heavenly Father-Mother, that He grant me a spirit of wisdom and revelation (of insight into mysteries and secrets) into the deep and intimate knowledge of the Divine by having the eyes of my heart flooded with light, that I may know and understand the hope to which He has called me and how rich is his glorious inheritance in me, and that I may know and understand the immeasurable, unlimited and surpassing greatness of His power as demonstrated in the working of His mighty strength.

Ephesians 3:14ff:

For this reason I bow my knees before God, my divine Father/Mother, that He grant me out of the rich treasury of His glory to be strengthened and reinforced with mighty power in my inner being by the Holy Spirit, Herself, which dwells in my innermost being and personality.

Adapted from Colossians 2:7:

(Place the name of the person for whom you are praying in the blanks.)

I pray that you, ___________, have the roots of your very being firmly planted in God's love, being continually built up in that love, abounding and overflowing in it with thankfulness. Amen.

Adapted from 2 Thessalonians 1:11:

I pray for you, ___________, that God fill you with goodness and power, complete for every task upon which you are called, and that your whole personality lean with trust and confidence on the goodness, love and power of God available to you, ___________. Amen.

Adapted from 1 Timothy 1:2:

To you, ___________, mercy and Mother, grace, spiritual blessing and favor as well as divine peace be yours from God, our heavenly Father/Mother. Amen.

Adapted from Acts 4:

Dearest Lord, stretch out your hand to cure ___________ as well as to perform signs and wonders through the power and authority given to me as your child. May _________ be aware of your Holy Spirit now operating in his/her life. Amen.

Inspirational Reading

Any number of good translations of the major scriptural texts of the world's religions can be purchased at most spiritual bookstores or over the Internet. Here are some sample titles, but if a particular edition is not available, another may do just as well. Following the scriptures is a list of general inspirational books.

Scriptural Texts

Chuang Tsu: Inner Chapters. Translated by Gia-fu Feng and Jane English. New York: Vintage, 1974.

The Koran. Translated by N.J. Dawood. Fifth revised edition. New York: Penguin, 1990.

Reps, Paul. *Zen Flesh, Zen Bones: A Collection of Zen and Pre-Zen Writings.* New York: Anchor Books, 1961.

The Rig Veda: An Anthology. Translated by Wendy O'Flaherty. New York: Penguin, 1981.

The Secret Teachings of Jesus: Four Gnostic Gospels. Translated by Marvin W. Meyer. New York: Random House, 1984.

Tao Te Ching. Translated by Stephen Mitchell. New York: HarperCollins, 1991.

World Scripture: A Comparative Anthology of Sacred Texts. Edited by Andrew Wilson. New York: Paragon House, 1995.

General Inspirational Books

Bastien, Peter E. *Praying with Martin Luther.* Winona, Minn.: St. Mary's Press, 1999.

Borg, Marcus, ed. *Jesus and Buddha: The Parallel Sayings.* Berkeley, Cal.: Seastone, 1997.

Brother Roger of Taizé. *No Greater Love: Sources of Taizé.* London, England: Geoffrey Chapman Mowbray, Wellington House, 1995. (Originally published in 1990.)

Casdorf, Richard, M.D., Ph.D. *The Miracles.* Plainfield, N.J.: Logos International, 1976.

Cataneo, Pascal. *Padre Pio Gleanings.* Translated by Maureen McCollum and Gabriel Dextraze. Sherbrook, Quebec: Editions Paulines, 1991.

Clement, Olivier. Taizé: *A Meaning to Life.* Chicago: GIA Publications, Inc., 1997.

Davis, Avram. *The Way of Flame: A Guide to the Forgotten Mystical Tradition of Jewish Meditation.* San Francisco: HarperSanFrancisco, 1996.

The Way of a Pilgrim and The Pilgrim Continues His Way. Trans. by R.M. French. San Francisco: HarperSanFrancisco, 1991.

Franciscan Friars of the Immaculate. *Padre Pio: The Wonder Worker.* Waite Park, Minn.: Park Press, Inc., 1999.

Higley, Connie and Alan. *Reference Guide for Essential Oils.* Olathe, Kans.: Abundant Health, 1998.

Hixon, Lex. *Mother of the Universe: Visions of the Goddess and Tantric Hymns of Enlightenment.* Wheaton, Ill.: Quest Books, 1994.

Huebsch, Bill. *Praying with Pope John XXIII.* Winona, Minn.: St. Mary's Press, 1999.

Jampolsky, Gerald G., M.D. *Forgiveness: The Greatest Healer of All.* Hillsboro, Or.: Beyond Words Publishing, Inc., 1999.

Mata, Sri Daya. *Enter the Quiet Heart: Creating a Loving Relationship with God.* Los Angeles: Self-Realization Fellowship, 1998.

Nouwen, Henri J. M. *The Only Necessary Thing: Living a Prayerful Life.* Compiled and edited by Wendy Wilson Greer. New York: Crossroad, 1999.

——. *Making All Things New: An Invitation to the Spiritual Life.* San Francisco: HarperSanFrancisco, 1981.

——. *Here and Now: Living in the Spirit.* New York: Crossroad, 1995.

——. *Life of the Beloved: Spiritual Living in a Secular World.* New York: Crossroad, 1992.

Occhiogrosso, Peter. *The Joy of Sects: A Spirited Guide to the World's Religious Traditions.* New York: Image, 1996.

Roth, Ron. *I Want to See Jesus in a New Light.* Carlsbad, Cal.: Hay House, 2000.

Roth, Ron, with Peter Occhiogrosso. *The Healing Path of Prayer: The Modern Mystic's Guide to Spiritual Power.* New York: Three Rivers, 1997.

——. *Prayer and the Five Stages of Healing*. Carlsbad, Cal.: Hay House, 1998.

Rumi, Jelaluddin. *The Ruins of the Heart*. Translated by Edmund Helminski. Putney, Vermont: Threshold, 1981.

——. *Unseen Rain*. Translated by John Moyne and Coleman Barks. Putney, Vermont: Threshold, 1986.

Schmidt, Joseph F. *Praying with Thérèse of Lisieux*. Winona, Minn.: Saint Mary's Press, 1992.

Stoutzenberger, Joseph M. and John D. Bohrer. *Praying with Francis of Assisi*. Winona, Minn., Saint Mary's Press, 1989.

Ward, Benedicta, S.L.G. *The Desert Christian: Sayings of the Desert Fathers*. New York: Macmillan, 1975.

Yogananda, Paramahansa. *In the Sancturary of the Soul: A Guide to Effective Prayer*. Los Angeles: Self-Realization Fellowship, 1998.

Please note: A new sacred oil that has been developed for Ron Roth will be available through the Celebrating Life Institute. For information, consult his Website at: **www.ronroth.com.**

About the Authors

Ron Roth, Ph.D., is an internationally known teacher, spiritual healer, and modern-day mystic. As a leading-edge voice bringing us into the New Millennium, he has appeared on many television and radio programs, including *The Oprah Winfrey Show.* Ron is the author of several books, including the bestseller *The Healing Path of Prayer,* and the audiocassette *Healing Prayers.* He served in the Roman Catholic priesthood for more than 25 years and is the founder of Celebrating Life Institute in Peru, Illinois, where he lives. You can contact Ron Roth at: **www.ronroth.com.**

Peter Occhiogrosso has been a journalist for 28 years and has written or co-written many books about religion and spirituality, including his guide to the world's great religious traditions, *The Joy of Sects.* He also co-authored *The Healing Path of Prayer* with Ron Roth. You can contact Peter at: **www.joyofsects.com.**

Other Hay House Titles of Related Interest

Books

The Experience of God,
edited by Jonathan Robinson

Experiencing the Soul, by Eliot Jay Rosen

God, Creation, and Tools for Life, by Sylvia Browne

Handle with Prayer, by Alan Cohen

The Jesus Code, by John Randolph Price

7 Paths to God, by Joan Borysenko, Ph.D.

Audios

All about God, a Dialogue Between Neale Donald Walsch and Deepak Chopra, M.D.

Healing with the Angels, by Doreen Virtue, Ph.D.

Pathways to God, a Dialogue Between Joan Borysenko, Ph.D., and Deepak Chopra, M.D.

We hope you enjoyed this Hay House book.
If you would like to receive a free catalog
featuring additional Hay House books and products,
or if you would like information about the
Hay Foundation, please contact:

Hay House, Inc.
P.O. Box 5100
Carlsbad, CA 92018-5100

(760) 431-7695 or **(800) 654-5126**
(760) 431-6948 (fax) or **(800) 650-5115 (fax)**

Please visit the Hay House Website at:
www.hayhouse.com